DISEASES

3rd Revised Edition

Volume 4

Fever to Hypothermia

Bryan Bunch
and
Jenny Tesar
EDITORS

GROLIER
an imprint of
SCHOLASTIC
Scholastic Library Publishing
www.scholastic.com/librarypublishing

Editors: Bryan Bunch and Jenny Tesar, Scientific Publishing

Design and production: G & H SOHO, Inc.
  Design: Gerry Burstein
  Prepress: Kathie Kounouklos

Writers:

Barbara Branca
Bryan Bunch
Barbara A. Darga
Betsy Feist
Gene R. Hawes
Wendy B. Murphy
Karin L. Rhines
Jenny Tesar
Bruce Wetterau
Gray Williams

Editorial assistant:
Marianne Bunch

Copyediting:
Felice Levy

Index
Felice Levy and Marianne Bunch

Creative assistance:
Pam Forde

Illustrators:

Photography supervisor:
Karin L. Rhines

Photographs:
Karin L. Rhines *(except where noted)*

Icons:
Steve Virkus and Karen Presser

Medical Illustrations:
Jean Cassels, Leslie Dunlap, Pamela Johnson, and Joel Snyder

Library of Congress Cataloging-in-Publication Data

Diseases / Bryan Bunch and Jenny Tesar, editors. — 3rd rev. ed.
      p. cm.
    Includes index.
    Summary: Alphabetically arranged articles presenting medical
  information on more than 500 diseases, discussing causes, symptoms,
  stages of the disease, its likelihood of striking, treatments, prevention,
  and long-term effects.
    ISBN 0-7172-6205-7 (set) — ISBN 0-7172-6206-5 (v. 1) — ISBN
  0-7172-6207-3 (v. 2) — ISBN 0-7172-6208-1 (v. 3) — ISBN 0-7172-6209-X
  (v. 4) — ISBN 0-7172-6210-3 (v. 5) — ISBN 0-7172-6211-1 (v. 6) — ISBN
  0-7172-6212-X (v. 7) — ISBN 0-7172-6213-8 (v. 8) 1. Diseases —
  Encyclopedias, Juvenile. I. Bunch, Bryan H. II. Tesar, Jenny E.

    R130.5.D57   2006
    616.003—dc22   2006007986

Third revised edition published 2006, by Scholastic Library Publishing.
First published in the United States in 1997 by
Grolier Educational, Sherman Turnpike, Danbury, CT 06816

Set ISBN-10: 0-7172-6205-7
Set ISBN-13: 978-0-7172-6205-2

Volume ISBN-10: 0-7172-6209-X
Volume ISBN-13: 978-0-7172-6209-0

Fever

SYMPTOM

Fever is defined as a body temperature elevated above normal, which is conventionally held to be 98.6°F on an oral thermometer or 99.8°F on a rectal thermometer. But there is considerable variation in normal body temperature depending on the individual, on the time of day (lowest around 4 a.m., highest around 6 p.m.), and on specific activities (resting, mild activity, strenuous exercise). A careful study in 1992 of 148 healthy college students found that their oral temperatures ranged from a low of 96.0°F in the morning to 99.9°F in the evening. Thus a fever is more accurately described as core body temperature elevated a degree or more above the individual's norm after relevant influences have been taken into account.

Virtually everyone experiences infection-induced fevers from time to time. Infants and toddlers are especially prone to fevers; they have limited immunity to the microorganisms encountered in life, and their temperature-regulation system is not yet fully formed.

Parts affected: Most fevers are part of the body's defense mechanism against bacterial or viral infection. Certain white blood cells respond to foreign invaders—an army of influenza viruses, for example—by releasing proteins called *pyrogens* (PIY-ruh-juhnz) into the bloodstream. These messengers travel to the temperature-control center of the brain, the hypothalamus, which activates various nerves in response. Some nerve impulses stimulate shivering, a form of muscle activity that generates heat. Other nerve impulses constrict blood vessels in the skin so that heat cannot easily escape the body. As a result body temperature rises. This higher temperature speeds up the operation of the immune response, so fever helps combat infection. Thus, so long as fevers do not reach extreme elevations or persist over an extended period, they are best left alone to do their work.

Associations: Many diseases are often accompanied by fever. These include influenza, mumps, measles, pneumonia, Lyme disease, blood poisoning (septicemia), and malaria. In young children even a mild cold can cause a feverish response. There

Emergency Room

Did You Know?

There are at least 100 different diseases and disorders that have fever as one of the symptoms.

Avoid aspirin

are also a number of rare or tropical diseases that have fever among the principal symptoms.

A fever may also occur as a symptom of noninfectious conditions, such as dehydration, heart attack, heat stroke, hypothermia, certain thyroid disorders, tumors of the lymphatic system, and such autoimmune diseases as "lupus" (systemic lupus erythematosus) and rheumatoid arthritis.

A physician must consider the whole range of symptoms to diagnose the root cause of a particular fever. For example, fever that comes on rapidly, rises to 104°F or higher, and is accompanied by severe headache, stiff neck, nausea and vomiting, and a strong reaction to light is part of a specific syndrome associated with bacterial meningitis, a medical emergency.

Related symptoms: Fevers typically are accompanied by headaches, shivering, sweating, chattering teeth, thirst, hot skin, rapid breathing, a flushed face, bodily aches and pains, and loss of appetite. Very high fevers (104°F or above) may cause confusion and hallucinations, especially in the young and the elderly; temperatures approaching 106°F and over may produce seizures and coma. People who have undergone a period of fever often feel fatigue, another feature of the body's recovery mechanisms.

Relief of symptoms: Temperature-lowering drugs such as aspirin or ibuprofen may be given to treat fevers due to infections. *In children or teenagers, however, do not use aspirin or medicines containing salicyclates to lower fever from virus infections, as they may provoke Reye's syndrome.* Avoid covering the patient with blankets, as the body needs to dissipate heat. Sponging or bathing with tepid water is helpful.

Dehydration often accompanies fever, so drinking plenty of water or other fluids is also recommended to ease discomfort—but avoid alcoholic or caffeine-based drinks; these actually promote dehydration. Soup is useful because sweating may have reduced salt levels in blood.

Prevention: Vaccination has reduced the incidence of some of the more dangerous fever-producing diseases.

History: In 1868 the German physician Carl Wunderlich was among the first to recognize that fever is a symptom and not a separate disease. He used the primitive thermometers then available to measure the armpit temperatures of, reportedly, 25,000 people.

In Germany the Celsius scale was standard. Wunderlich found that the average of his measurements was 37°C to the nearest degree. This is the apparent source of the commonly used 98.6°F for normal, since 37°C exactly equals 98.6°F.

Fever blister   *See* **Cold sore**

Fibrillation, ventricular   *See* **Ventricular fibrillation**

Fibrocystic breast disease
(FIY-broh-SIHS-tihk)

DISORDER

TYPE: HORMONAL

See also
Breast cancer
Cysts
Hormonal system
Ovaries

On the Internet
MEDLINE PLUS
www.nlm.nih.gov/medlineplus/
ency/article/000912.htm

It is common for women to find lumps in their breasts. The great majority of these lumps are not cancerous. Rather, they are indications of fibrocystic breast disease. The name is a misnomer since the condition, also known as *cystic mastitis*, is not really a disease. Treatment is seldom required. However, women with fibrocystic breast disease should be monitored by a physician since the condition is considered a risk factor for breast cancer.

Parts affected: Women with fibrocystic breast disease develop cysts in their breasts. A cyst is a sac filled with fluid. Characteristically, multiple cysts of various sizes occur in both breasts of affected women.

Cause: Hormones produced by the ovaries appear to be involved in development of fibrocystic breast disease. As estrogen levels rise during the menstrual cycle, the breast cysts become larger and more tender.

Incidence: Fibrocystic breast disease is the most common disorder of women's breasts. Some 60% of women, mostly premenopausal women over 30, experience this condition. New cysts generally do not develop after menopause.

Noticeable symptoms: The main symptom of fibrocystic breast disease is a lumpy quality to the breasts. The lumps may be accompanied by breast pain or tenderness. Because it is difficult to feel the difference between cancerous and noncancer-

Phone doctor

ous lumps, any woman who detects a lump should see a physician as soon as possible.

Diagnosis: A physician will perform an examination and order mammogram or ultrasound photographs of the breasts. Often, a *biopsy* is necessary to determine whether the cysts are benign or cancerous. In this procedure a small amount of fluid is removed from a cyst and examined under a microscope.

Prevention and possible actions: A physician may recommend that a patient limit consumption of certain substances that have been linked to fibrocystic breast disease. These include dietary fat; caffeinated beverages such as coffee, tea, and cola; chocolate; and alcohol. Treatment is seldom required for fibrocystic breast disease. Some patients improve when fat is reduced to 25% of total calories and caffeine is eliminated completely from the diet. Sometimes birth control pills eliminate the cysts.

All women age 30 and older should examine their breasts once a month (see illustration at breast cancer entry). The examination should be done five to seven days after the menstrual period ends. The breast tissue is less likely to be lumpy at this time. An annual mammogram is recommended for women with fibrocystic breast disease.

Fibromyalgia
(FIY-bruh-miy-AAL-jee-uh)

DISEASE

TYPE: UNKNOWN

On the Internet
FIBROMYALGIA NETWORK
www.fmnetnews.com/pages/
basics.html

Millions of Americans experience pain at specific locations on the neck, chest, back, hips, and thighs day in and day out. Sometimes the pain is so severe that they cannot carry out normal activities. These individuals have fibromyalgia.

Cause: The cause of fibromyalgia is unknown. Since there are no objective tests, such as measures of blood pressure or antibody activity, some physicians may consider fibromyalgia to be psychosomatic (symptoms produced by the mind).

Incidence: About 4 million Americans and half a million Canadians have been diagnosed as having fibromyalgia. Most people with fibromyalgia experience the earliest symptoms between 20 and 50 years of age. Most are women, but men can also have fibromyalgia. Older people with similar symptoms may have an unrelated autoimmune disease called polymyalgia rheumatica (POL-ee-miy-AAL-jee-uh roo-MAAT-ihk-uh).

Noticeable symptoms: Deep body pain that typically is symmetrical—for example, if there is pain in one shoulder, then it exists in the other as well—is the main symptom. The pain can be mild or intense; it may spread from one area of the body to another. Difficulty in sleeping, stiffness on awakening, and anxiety may also be present. The pain may be mild in the morning but get worse as the day goes on.

Diagnosis: If fibromyalgia is suspected, a physician will press on specific spots on both sides of the neck, chest, shoulders, hips, and thighs. These are called tender points. If 11 of these 18 tender points are painful, the cause of the pain is probably fibromyalgia. The tender points are places in the body where muscles attach to tendons or bones. The pain begins in the soft tissues—tendons and ligaments—not in the muscles themselves.

Treatment: Daily low-impact aerobic exercises such as walking and swimming can help relieve the pain. Jogging and weight lifting are not recommended. Mild antidepressants and painkillers can help with sleeping difficulties, anxiety, and pain. Relaxation exercises can also reduce symptoms.

Fifth disease

DISEASE

TYPE: INFECTIOUS (VIRAL)

> **Did You Know?**
> The original "fourth disease" was a rash named Filatov-Dukes' disease, which today most physicians think is just misdiagnosed second or third disease (scarlet fever or rubella).

The scientific name for fifth disease is *erythema infectiosum* (EHR-uh-THEE-muh ihn-fehk-tee-OH-sum), which means "infectious redness." The common name is fifth disease because this was the fifth of the childhood viral rash diseases (such as measles and rubella) to be identified.

Fifth disease is a very common and usually mild infection; it often produces no noticeable symptoms at all. The disease temporarily suppresses the production of red blood cells until the immune system overcomes the virus. Its most distinctive feature is an intensely red facial rash that makes it look as if the skin had been sharply slapped.

Most of those who catch fifth disease suffer no adverse consequences. But a minority—individuals with weakened immune systems or blood diseases and women who are pregnant—may be at greater risk.

Cause: Fifth disease is caused by Parvovirus B19, a virus that affects only human beings. It is carried in exhaled droplets of

On the Internet
KIDS HEALTH
kidshealth.org/parent/infections/
bacterial_viral/fifth.html

moisture from the nose and throat, and spreads easily and quickly among individuals in close contact with one another, such as family members and schoolchildren.

Incidence: Because the virus is so easily spread, it is extremely common and occurs most frequently in children. At least half of all adults over the age of 20 are believed to have had the disease, often without knowing it.

Noticeable symptoms: As the immune system reacts to destroy the virus, the infected person may experience mild flu-like symptoms such as headache, fatigue, and perhaps a slight fever. The distinctive facial rash appears about a week later. There may also be a slightly bumpy and itchy rash on the body. By this time, however, the person is no longer infectious. Adults are likely to experience symptoms of arthritis that may linger for weeks after the infection has otherwise vanished.

Diagnosis: Usually, the appearance of the facial rash is sufficient for diagnosis. Scarlet fever, with a similar rash, produces a high fever; this does not occur with fifth disease. A blood test will reveal antibodies to the virus produced by the immune system.

Treatment options and outlook: Like most infections caused by viruses, fifth disease cannot be treated with antibiotics or other medications but must run its course until the immune system overcomes it. The antibodies produced by the immune system convey permanent immunity from future infection.

Stages and progress: The rash on the face is likely to spread downward to the trunk and limbs. There it tends to be blotchy and less vivid in color. The rash often looks lacy or netted in its later stages. It fades and recurs for one to three weeks until it finally disappears. In adolescents and adults the rash may cause itching, but children may experience no discomfort at all.

Risk factors: Those who have significantly weakened immune systems, such as AIDS patients or organ transplant recipients, may be more severely affected, and the prolonged suppression of red blood cells may result in dangerous anemia. Also at risk are individuals with blood disorders, such as sickle cell anemia or leukemia, who depend on high rates of red-cell production. A woman who becomes infected during pregnancy may transmit the infection to the fetus, raising the risk of miscarriage or stillbirth.

See **Elephantiasis**

Finger and toenail fungus

DISEASE

TYPE: INFECTIOUS (FUNGAL)

See also
Fungus diseases
Nail infections and injuries

Did You Know?

Physicians often examine fingernails as part of a diagnosis since their appearance can reveal anemia, overactive thyroid, lung diseases, psoriasis, and/or vitamin deficiency.

A chronic but usually painless condition, fungus infection of fingernails or toenails can turn nails white, yellow, gray, brown, or black and deform them as well. The most usual form is called *onychomycosis* (ON-ih-koh-miy-KOH-sihs).

Cause: Any of several types of fungus can cause long-term inflammation of the nails on the fingers or toes—more often on the toes than the fingers.

Noticeable symptoms: There usually is no pain with a fungal infection; discoloration and thickening of nails are the most obvious symptoms. Affected nails lose their luster and become opaque and brittle. There may be bumpy ridges called striations, a worm-eaten appearance, or flaking of a nail surface. The fungus may spread to surrounding skin, causing white, flaky patches. In some cases the nail tends to separate from the fingertip or toe.

Treatment options: The fungus rarely clears on its own. Several oral antifungal medications are available but they are not always effective, need to be taken for months, and can have troublesome side effects. Most drugs applied directly to the nail do not kill deep-lying fungus. If the problem is not causing great distress, a physician may suggest living with it.

Prevention: Keep hands and feet clean and dry as much as possible. Wear gloves when your hands must be in water for any extended period. Do not use artificial fingernails. Wear properly fitted shoes. Do not walk barefoot in public places.

Fitness

DISEASE

See also
Exercise
Obesity

Keeping physically fit has been extensively documented to be an important part of wellness. It keeps the heart and muscles strong, improves balance and flexibility, and helps ward off many disorders and illnesses. To determine a person's current fitness status and to establish a baseline from which to gauge progress, various fitness tests are conducted. Fitness tests can help in designing an appropriate, realistic exercise program for a person, in monitoring the person's progress and, if necessary,

On the Internet
KIDS HEALTH
kidshealth.org/teen/exercise/
index.html

Phone doctor

fine-tuning the program. Many programs can easily be done at home or on community tracks or playgrounds.

Athletes make fitness tests a regular part of their conditioning regime, and organizations such as law-enforcement groups require applicants to meet certain levels on such tests. Schools also have designed fitness tests for their students. Each test has a range of desirable scores. For example, a 14-year-old girl might be expected to be able to do 30 to 48 partial curl-ups and to complete a one-mile walk/run in 8.5 to 11 minutes. Boys generally are expected to have higher scores. In the same situation, a 14-year-old boy's goal would be 40 to 62 partial curl-ups and completing a one-mile walk/run in 7 to 9.5 minutes. Goals for younger children are lower; those for older teens are higher. As an adult ages, goals decline. For example, a good score for women 18 to 25 in a 1-minute sit-up test is 37 to 43 sit-ups; by the time women are 65 or older, a good score is 17 to 23. ***Important: Some tests may not be appropriate for people of a certain age or for people with certain medical conditions. Check with your physician prior to any fitness testing.***

Test results do not always give a true picture of a person's fitness, or of how he or she compares with the norm. Standardizing techniques—as in a jump test—can be difficult. Small inaccuracies in measurement can give large variations in results. Some tests may overestimate or underestimate conditions; for example, using waist circumference as an indication of fat inside the abdominal wall may overestimate health risk in tall individuals and underestimate risk in short people.

There are five basic categories of fitness tests, listed here with examples of standard tests:

Body composition: These tests are often part of a general physical examination. They include measurements of height, weight, girths, and body fat. The body mass index (described in the entry on obesity) is a good indicator of a person's risk of poor health but not ideal for measuring body fat. A better tool is the skinfold test, which estimates body fat by measuring skinfold thickness on anywhere from three to nine different places on the body. Other fitness tests that may be part of general physical exams measure resting heart rate, pulse, and lung capacity.

Strength and power: These tests are designed to measure upper-body, abdominal, and lower-body strength. The number of sit-ups, curl-ups, or partial curl-ups performed in one minute

The V-sit is a common test of physical fitness. It measures the flexibility of the lower back and hamstrings. Scores based on how far the person can reach are measured in inches.

indicates abdominal strength. Pull-ups and a medicine-ball throw illustrate arm and upper-body strength. A device called a dynamometer tests handgrip strength. Measurements taken on gym equipment indicate the strength of specific muscle groups. A vertical jump test, often part of a basketball player's or other athlete's fitness testing, measures how high a person can jump. The test can be conducted off two legs, one leg, with a step into the jump, or with a run-up, depending on the sport involved.

Flexibility: A simple sit-and-reach test, which involves learning forward as far as possible while sitting on the floor with legs straight ahead, measures hamstring and lower-back mobility. One test of shoulder flexibility involves holding a stick in front of the body with both hands, then lifting the stick over the head to behind the neck. Goniometers and flexometers are instruments that measure range of motion at a joint.

Endurance and stamina: The length of time needed to run or walk a specified distance is an indication of aerobic (cardiopulmonary) power. A treadmill test also determines aerobic power; it is often used for people with suspected cardiovascular disease. A popular assessment of how efficiently muscle cells burn food to produce mechanical energy—an indication of anaerobic performance—is the Wingate test. It is based on cycling at maximum speed for 30 seconds.

Speed: Tests that measure speed are of particular interest to athletes. A common test consists of timed sprints over distances of 50 to 300 feet.

"Flu"

See **Gastroenteritis; Influenza; "Virus" infection**

Food poisoning

REFERENCE

Food poisoning refers to a group of illnesses caused by eating contaminated or naturally poisonous foods. Some of these illnesses produce relatively minor discomfort and clear up without medical treatment in a matter of hours. Others, such as botulism or mushroom poisoning, can make a person very ill and even be fatal without prompt medical treatment.

Bacterial food poisoning: Bacteria of many types live on all but sterilized surfaces, and they multiply with extreme rapidity. The most common sources of dangerous bacteria, however, are feces or

On the Internet
CENTERS FOR DISEASE CONTROL
AND PREVENTION (CDC)
www.cdc.gov/ncidod/dbmd/
diseaseinfo/
foodborneinfections_g.htm

Did You Know?

In 1795 French emperor
Napoleon I offered a prize
for a better way to preserve
food. The contest was won
by Nicolas-Francis Appert,
who stopped decay by
heating food above boiling
and then sealing it in airtight
containers—a method we
now call canning.

soil. Bacteria are also found in or on animal products, usually as a result of handling practices that allow intestinal material to come into contact with meat that is intended to be eaten. Pasteurization destroys most bacteria, but unpasteurized milk can contain tuberculosis or brucellosis bacteria.

Staphylococcus aureus, known as "staph," and *Salmonella* are bacteria that can grow on many different kinds of food. Contamination usually starts when a prepared dish slowly cools at room temperature for an extended period. Other bacteria that produce diarrhea include *Campylobacter, Shigella,* and *Yersinia*. The gastric distress generally clears up in a few hours without treatment.

Some bacterial food poisoning is deadly. *Listeria monocytogenes* causes about 28% of all food poisoning deaths. The bacteria tolerate cold, acidic solutions, salt, and nitrites. They can contaminate a wide array of foods, primarily unpasteurized milk, ice cream, soft cheeses, hot dogs, raw meats and poultry, and even fresh vegetables. *Escherichia coli* 0157:H7 (a variety of *E. coli*) is best known as the cause of food poisoning linked to undercooked hamburgers contaminated with animal manure; other foods, even apple cider, can be similarly contaminated. The toxin causes bloody diarrhea and, in young children and the elderly, can lead to death from severe anemia and kidney failure within a few days.

Vibrio vulnificus can be found in oysters, clams, and other shellfish harvested from warm ocean waters. Contaminated shellfish eaten raw or improperly cooked causes the sudden onset of diarrhea, vomiting, and abdominal pain. Patients with liver or other chronic diseases may suffer fatal complications.

Clostridia bacteria, the cause of botulism, cannot tolerate oxygen, but can grow in canned foods or foods otherwise stored in a low-oxygen environment. Eating even a small amount of contaminated food can produce life-threatening paralysis.

Viral contamination: People who eat raw shellfish, such as clams or oysters, risk the virus hepatitis A if the food was illegally harvested in sewage-contaminated waters. Norwalk viruses and related strains also contaminate raw or improperly cooked shellfish, as well as salad vegetables, and cause upward of two-thirds of all cases of food poisoning. These viruses are spread by food contaminated with traces of human fecal matter. Symptoms include nausea and vomiting, abdominal pain, and diarrhea, which in some cases may be bloody. Symptoms usually disappear in one to three days.

Toxic tides: In addition to viruses, blue-green algae or protists that live in water can contaminate fish or shellfish. The fish or shellfish often survive unharmed. However, the toxins, which are seldom destroyed by cooking, can be deadly to humans, although more often they produce gastrointestinal disorders, respiratory problems, confusion, or memory loss. The organisms that cause this poisoning can grow in such profusion that they turn seawater red, brown, or green—blooms sometimes called "toxic tides."

Emergency Room

Naturally poisonous foods: About 80 kinds of wild mushrooms are poisonous. Mushroom poisoning causes convulsions, nausea, vomiting, vision problems, and stupor. ***Get immediate medical attention if you suspect that you have eaten a poisonous mushroom.***

Berries and leaves should never be eaten unless you are certain about their safety. Even parts of domesticated fruits and vegetables can be poisonous, including potato eyes and sprouts, rhubarb leaves, and peach pits.

Incidence: In the United States alone there are about 76 million cases of food poisoning each year, leading to about 5,000 deaths. Worldwide, 7 to 8 million persons die annually.

Wash hands

Prevention: Bacterial food poisoning can usually be prevented by following safe practices in the kitchen. For example, always wash your hands with soap and water before *and* after handling food. That prevents spreading bacteria to food and spreading bacteria from food to you (such as salmonella from raw eggs). Clean the sink and countertops regularly with a detergent containing bleach.

Defrost frozen meats in the refrigerator or a microwave. Cook meats thoroughly—juices should run clear and centers should be brown, not pink. Wrap and refrigerate all leftovers quickly, and always refrigerate stuffing from poultry in a separate container. Ready-to-eat meats that have been in the refrigerator for a couple of weeks may not be safe to eat because *Listeria* bacteria can grow even in cold conditions.

Throw away food in poorly sealed containers or swollen cans, or food that smells or looks odd or is moldy (except cheese, which can be trimmed of mold safely). Because of *Salmonella*

Simple steps halt most food poisoning before it can happen. Meat surfaces often are contaminated, so a different cutting board should be used to trim or cut meat from the one used for vegetables. This is especially important if the vegetables are to be eaten raw. Bacteria or viruses on the outer surfaces of meat are almost always destroyed in the cooking process. All cutting boards should be washed with soap and hot water after they have been used.

outbreaks, many food authorities recommend that you not eat cracked eggs or foods prepared with uncooked eggs—for example, a traditional Caesar salad or chocolate mousse.

Foot problems

REFERENCE

Most people walk an average of 10,000 steps every day and will probably walk the equivalent of four and a half times around Earth—115,000 miles in all—during a lifetime. With each step the foot's 26 bones and assorted muscles, tendons, and ligaments absorb a tremendous amount. But feet are made for it. Their arching bones distribute weight outward from the heels toward the toes; the soles of the feet are cushioned by a thick pad of fibrous tissue and fat known as the plantar fascia (PLAAN-tuhr FAASH-ee-uh). For some, though, corns or blisters, foot diseases such as athlete's foot, or inherited conditions cause discomfort. Some chronic illnesses also affect the feet--diabetes and arthritis, for example.

Calluses and corns: Chafing and pressure on the foot can lead to a callus, a thick pad of dead skin usually found on the ball of the foot or under the heel. Corns are highly concentrated calluses that build up in response to rubbing and pressure.

When calluses or corns get big enough, they begin pressing on nerves, causing pain and inflammation. You can treat the problem by covering the site with an unmedicated moleskin pad or a

On the Internet

AMERICAN ACADEMY
OF FAMILY PHYSICIANS
familydoctor.org/x2574.xml

small "donut ring" to protect against scraping. Using a moisturizing cream on your feet often helps. If the problem persists, consult your doctor.

Painful heel syndrome: About 3 million people each year—most of them over 40—suffer painful heel syndrome, officially known as *plantar fasciitis* (FAASH-ee-IY-tihs). The plantar fascia extends along the bottom of the foot and is attached to the toes and heel bone. As people get older, the plantar fascia becomes less flexible, tending to shorten when the foot is resting. Walking long distances, jogging on hard surfaces, or overusing the feet causes inflammation of the plantar fascia. The pain in the heel typically begins when taking the first few steps after a night's sleep or otherwise resting the foot. Often this condition is termed a *heel spur,* since it feels like a bump on the heel pressing against a nerve— real heel spurs may or may not cause pain, however.

Regular foot-stretching exercises repeated daily usually help prevent painful heel syndrome. Grasp the toes and pull each foot separately back toward the shin four or five times, holding it as far back as is comfortable for several seconds each time. Cutting back on activities that put stress on the heel also helps. Supportive, well-cushioned shoes with low heels are recommended. Check with a podiatrist before using any type of heel cushion insert.

Bunions and hammertoes: A bunion occurs when the big toe angles inward so that it points toward the little toe, causing the metatarsal (MEHT-uh-TAHR-suhl) bone in the foot to stick out at the base of the big toe joint. This causes a bump at the base of the big toe—a bunion. The misalignment is progressive. If left untreated, a bunion can become so painful as to interfere with walking and even standing. The best remedy is surgery to realign the bone.

Hammertoes occur when the middle joint of the second toe—or sometimes the third or fourth toe—grows downward instead of straight ahead. This pushes the joint upward, where it rubs against the shoe and becomes inflamed. One possible cause is nerve damage from diabetes mellitus. Soft-soled shoes with plenty of toe room can help relieve the irritation. Protective pads and an orthotic also help, but surgery may be needed to correct a severe case.

Flat feet: With this disorder the natural arch formed by bones of the feet flattens out—hence the other name, *fallen arches*. The soles rest entirely on the ground when standing. Flat feet can be hereditary, but they also may be caused by some medical conditions, including obesity, rickets, and metabolic disorders. Fallen arches can cause considerable pain in the feet, calves, and even the lower back due to the resulting misalignment of bones. A podiatrist may prescribe arch supports to correct flat feet. Treatment may also include a program of exercise.

Fractures, dislocations, sprains, and strains

A fall, a collision of any kind, and many other types of accidents may create damage to bones, joints, or muscles. Often internal structures must be imaged to know if a serious injury has occurred. Such injuries are classed primarily by whether they affect a bone, joint, or muscle.

- *Fractures* result whenever a bone is hit by enough force to make it break, creating either a small crack or, in a serious fracture, a complete break.
- *Dislocations* occur when bone has slipped out of its normal position in a joint where two bones meet.
- *Sprains* affect the ligaments in a joint. Usually, a sudden twisting of the knee or elbow causes this type of injury. A sprain may result from overstretching or from small tears on the edges of a ligament. A complete parting is usually called a *torn ligament*.
- *Strains*—also called *muscle pulls*—are the most common and usually the mildest of the three injuries. Overworking or overextending muscles, doing heavy exercise during cold weather, and even failing to drink enough fluids can lead to small tears that make using muscles painful.
- Torn, severed, or irritated tendons, the tissues that connect muscles to bones, are also common and are considered in separate entries.

Fractures: There are two basic types of fractures, open and closed. The *open fracture*—also called a *compound fracture*—is generally more serious because in this type bone has broken through the skin. The break causes considerable damage to surrounding tissue and can cause serious bleeding if a large artery is broken. The broken bone is also exposed to infection.

Almost any problem that cracks or breaks a bone is the result of a fall or hard blow. Falls and external twisting can cause sprains or dislocations. Strains result from misuse of muscles.

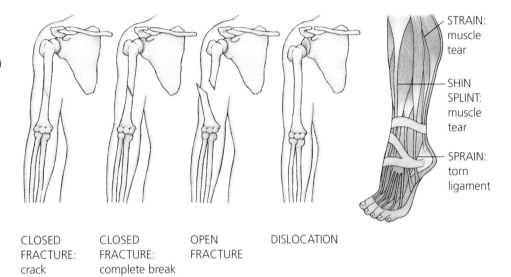

CLOSED FRACTURE: crack

CLOSED FRACTURE: complete break

OPEN FRACTURE

DISLOCATION

STRAIN: muscle tear

SHIN SPLINT: muscle tear

SPRAIN: torn ligament

On the Internet
NEW YORK ONLINE ACCESS TO HEALTH
www.noah-health.org/en/bjm/fractures/

Emergency Room

A *closed fracture* may be either a crack in a bone or a complete break, but in either case the skin is not broken. But even when bone does not break the skin it can cause serious internal damage. A skull fracture that causes pressure on the brain or a broken rib that pierces a lung can be life-threatening.

Bones that most often break include those of the collar, foot, leg, hand, wrist, and arm. The elderly fracture more easily than younger people because bones become weaker and more brittle with age—in severe cases this tendency becomes the disorder osteoporosis. A broken hip resulting from a fall is common among older people, especially those with osteoporosis. Although there are several types of painful fractures of bones in the spine, including the neck, the main danger is not from fracture of bone but from damage to the spinal cord.

Fractures usually produce severe pain. The injured region probably swells, and in complete breaks a finger, arm, or leg may look deformed. ***See your doctor immediately whenever you suspect a fracture, even if you think it is minor.***

After taking x-rays, the physician will realign broken bones that are out of normal position. Ordinarily, a doctor will align the bones from outside the body and immobilize broken fingers, arms, or legs with rigid devices (*splints*) held in place with a bandage, with a plaster restraining tube called a *cast,* or with an inflated restraint, also called a cast. Splints or casts may have to be worn for several weeks while the body repairs the break and restores strength to the bones. Some fractures, such as that of a collarbone, may require only immobilization with an arm holder called a *sling*. The most severe fractures may require surgery to reset the bones into their proper place, or the doctor may decide it is best to brace a broken bone internally with metal screws, rods, or plates.

Phone doctor

Dislocations: A finger, thumb, or shoulder bone may be pulled out of a joint, usually by a fall or physical blow. Such a dislocation may damage ligaments and other tissues in the joint, which soon become misshapen, swollen, and the source of intense pain. ***Get medical help as soon as possible.*** A doctor may be able to quickly realign the bones if internal damage is not serious and swelling has not gone too far. Only someone with proper training should realign dislocated bones, however. Otherwise, further damage may result.

The joint will be immobilized with a cast or other device for about two weeks to allow ligaments and other tissues time to heal. Surgery may be necessary to repair severely damaged tissues. Joints may also be partly dislocated, a condition called *subluxation* (sub-luk-SAY-shuhn). Usually partial dislocations pop back into position, leaving a trail of damage that produces symptoms similar to those of a complete dislocation but requiring no special treatment.

Sprains: Any ligaments holding bones or cartilage together at a joint can be twisted, torn, or otherwise damaged by a fall or other impact. Ankles, knees, and finger joints are regularly subjected to force in daily use, so their ligaments tend to get sprained most often.

A sprain's severity depends on how much damage has been done to the ligament. Stretching and small tears produce a mild sprain. They make the joint painful to move but still able to function. When ligaments are *ruptured*—completely torn— the sprain is severe. There will usually be swelling and pain, and depending on the extent to which the ligaments are torn, the joint may look deformed.

For mild sprains wrap the joint with an elastic bandage, and use an ice pack periodically during the first day or two to help keep swelling down. Start exercising the joint gently after a day or two of rest and ice packs. Try strengthening the ligament slowly without forcing it to take weight too soon. Keeping the damaged joint elevated when possible helps reduce swelling.

See a doctor for a severe sprain or if milder pain continues for more than two to three days. If x-rays show severe tearing of the ligament, the doctor may recommend surgery to repair the damage. Otherwise, the treatment may be nothing more than a splint or cast to immobilize the joint while ligaments heal.

Strains: Muscle fibers tear when subjected to excess exertion or stretching. You will probably feel some immediate pain if you tear a muscle by, say, lifting a heavy weight or suddenly reaching out to catch a baseball. Later the muscle will gradually become swollen, tender, and stiff.

Muscle strains nearly always heal completely by themselves within a few days. However, if you do not treat a serious muscle strain properly, or if you strain the muscle repeatedly, you may lose strength in the muscle permanently. If the muscle will not function after a strain, it may be completely torn. See a doctor in that case.

For minor muscle strains an ice pack can help ease the pain and keep swelling down. An elastic bandage wrapped around the affected area also reduces swelling, but the bandage must not be so tight that it hampers blood circulation.

If the pain or swelling is severe, get medical treatment. A doctor may recommend surgery for muscles that are torn completely. If the damage is less severe, a physician may prescribe medication for pain and tell you to rest the muscle.

You can usually prevent strains by doing warmup exercises to get blood flowing to muscles and to increase muscle flexibility.

Overuse injuries: Athletes or joggers may suffer *stress fractures* of foot and leg bones. Usually, these cracks are so small they do not even show on an x-ray, but they can be quite painful. Caused by repetitive pounding against hard surfaces, stress fractures heal with sufficient rest.

Runners may develop *shin splints,* a pain in the front of the lower leg. The shin splint may be caused by a minor muscle tear, a stress fracture of the bone, or an inflammation of the tissue covering the shinbone. Swollen muscles pressing against blood vessels (called *anterior compartment syndrome*) also cause shin splints. Resting for a week or two usually clears up the disorder.

Phone doctor

Fragile X syndrome

DISEASE

TYPE: GENETIC

See also
Developmental disability
Genetic diseases
Genome
Hemophilias
Huntington's disease

On the Internet
NATIONAL FRAGILE X
FOUNDATION
www.fragilex.org/html/
home.shtml

Developmental disability (mental retardation) is a feature of several X-linked (or sex-linked) genetic disorders. These are caused by defective genes in the X chromosome and affect either boys only or more boys than girls. By far the most common form of X-linked developmental disability is fragile X syndrome. Boys who have this defect in their single X chromosome are strongly affected. Girls who have the defect in one of their two X chromosomes tend to be less affected or show no signs of the disorder at all.

Cause: Like several other genetic defects fragile X syndrome results from an abnormal number of repetitions of a normal sequence that is part of the genetic code. Somewhat unexpectedly, the abnormal repetitions do not develop in a single generation.

The normal number of repetitions of this sequence for the affected gene, known as the *FMRI* gene, is about 30. A spontaneous mutation may cause this number to expand to 50 or more—a condition called a *premutation* since it does not usually produce any observable traits. But the number of repetitions may continue to increase through one or more further generations until it reaches 200 or more. At that point the repetitions interfere with the function of the gene, causing fragile X syndrome. The name comes from the tendency of the repeated fragment to cause the X chromosome to bend or break.

Incidence: Fragile X syndrome appears in about 1 of every 1,500 boys, and 1 of every 2,500 girls, making it the second-ranked cause of developmental disability (after Down syndrome).

Noticeable symptoms: Developmental disability is usually apparent by early childhood. Many boys with fragile X syndrome have characteristic facial features: large, protruding ears and a long face with a prominent forehead and chin.

Diagnosis: Tests of DNA can identify not only the large number of repetitions in a full fragile X mutation but also the limited number of repetitions in a premutation. Thus, testing can identify both affected individuals and "carrier" parents.

Treatment and outlook: Special education and a sheltered environment can help affected individuals lead a meaningful and productive life. Medications can reduce some of the behavioral problems associated with the condition, such as wide mood swings and hyperactivity.

Freckles

See **Moles and freckles**

Frostbite

Emergency Room

Exposure of the skin to extreme cold can freeze parts of the body, a condition known as frostbite. The fingers, toes, nose, and ears are the body parts most commonly affected.

Cause: When a person is exposed to very cold temperatures for a prolonged period of time, ice crystals form within and between the cells of the skin and underlying tissue. The flow of blood to the exposed area slows or even stops. If blood flow ceases entirely, it can result in gangrene, caused by death of the affected tissue. People with circulatory problems such as atherosclerosis or Raynaud's disease have an increased risk of frostbite. Alcohol and tobacco smoking contribute to frostbite by also interfering with circulation.

Noticeable symptoms: At first the skin will turn red and may be painful. As frostbite develops, the skin will feel very cold. It may turn white and feel numb. Blisters may form. If tissue dies, it will turn black.

At the first signs of frostbite, go indoors. Place a warm cloth over the affected area. Never massage or immerse the area in hot or cold water. As the skin rewarms, it turns red and becomes painful. Swelling may occur. *If sensation and normal coloring do not return within a short time, seek immediate medical attention.*

Treatment options: After an examination to determine the extent of frostbite, a doctor will take measures to rewarm the body without further damaging tissue. Running water just above body temperature is useful, although painful. Although warm drinks may seem helpful, they usually are not. Avoid drinks with caffeine or alcohol and smoking. Bed rest, antibiotics, and a tetanus injection may be necessary.

Prevention: Most cases of frostbite can be prevented by wearing proper clothing in cold conditions. If you normally live in a

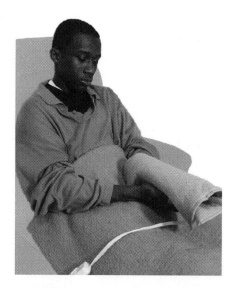

At the first sign of frostbite, get out of the cold and move somewhere warm. If hands or feet are red and feel cold to the touch, they should be warmed slowly by covering with a blanket or using a heating pad set at its lowest setting or by immersing the exremity in water that is just above body temperature. If the skin has begun to turn white, however, do not try to rewarm but keep the victim from moving parts affected until medical help arrives.

Avoid alcohol

warmer climate, give your body—in particular, your circulatory system—time to adjust to the change. At first remain in the cold for only brief periods of time. Over several days gradually increase the time. ***Do not consume alcohol if you expect to be exposed to prolonged cold.***

Fungus diseases

REFERENCE

It is easy, but misleading, to think of the mushroom as a typical fungus. Most funguses are tiny creatures somewhat like bacteria in size and functioning. Fungus diseases result from damage to bodily tissue inflicted by the action of these microscopic funguses. More than 100,000 species of funguses have been identified. They include mildews, molds, mushrooms, and yeasts. Most funguses are harmless or beneficial; for example, some are essential to the production of bread, alcoholic beverages, and many antibiotics.

Cause: Fungus diseases arise when conditions are suitable for fungal growth—typically, in moist regions of the body, ranging from places where skin is pressed against skin (such as between toes) to interior regions such as the mouth or lungs. A few funguses can grow on any skin surface, especially if protected from sunlight. Funguses produce illnesses in the same way that bacteria do, either by using parts of cells for nutrients or by releasing toxins. Some funguses also cause allergic reactions.

On the Internet
MERCK MANUAL OF DIAGNOSIS
AND THERAPY
www.merck.com/mrkshared/
mmanual/section13/
chapter158/158a.jsp

Bacteria can help protect against fungus diseases. Often, when a person reduces the bacterial population with antibiotics, funguses normally present on skin take advantage of the decreased competition and increase, causing mild skin diseases. Usually, when the antibiotic treatment is over, bacteria return and the skin goes back to normal.

Incidence: Large majorities of children and adults develop minor fungus diseases at one time or another. Instances of more serious varieties of fungus diseases, which can affect the lungs or other organs, are comparatively rare in developed countries among persons otherwise in good health. The incidence of fungus infection tends to be higher among individuals whose bodily defenses have been weakened by other diseases, including diabetes mellitus and AIDS.

Mild fungus diseases: The common skin fungus infections each have separate entries in this set, including candidiasis and several different forms of *tinea* (TIHN-ee-uh)—athlete's foot, finger and toenail fungus, jock itch, and ringworm.

Tinea infections are usually contagious, but a form called *tinea versicolor* (VUR-sih-KUHL-uhr) is caused by funguses normally present on the skin of most individuals. Such funguses are thought to multiply in sites where skin glands are concentrated, leaving scaly or pink regions that discolor the chest, neck, upper arms, back, and even the face. Mild tinea versicolor can be eliminated by shampoos used to control dandruff, but some infections require prescription antifungal medicines.

Rare fungus diseases: There are many other fungus diseases that are more disabling but far less common than tinea or candidiasis. In many cases these diseases infect the lungs through inhalation.

Aspergillosis (AAS-puhr-juh-LOH-sihs): Aspergillosis is marked by the development of fibrous masses in the lungs. Inhalation of fungal spores, which abound on rotting vegetation, combined with a compromised immune system is believed to be the cause of the lung disease. The same fungus can also provoke an allergic reaction.

Blastomycosis (BLAAS-toh-miy-KOH-sihs): Blastomycosis infects the lungs, causing symptoms similar to those of pneumonia, but it can spread to other organs. It results from inhalation of spores found in soil. The disease responds quickly to antifungal medicine in most cases.

Coccidioidomycosis (kok-SIHD-ee-OI-doh-miy-KOH-sihs) is the official name for valley fever.

Cryptococcosis (KRIHP-tuh-koh-KOH-sis): The disease cryptococcosis typically leads to lesions in the lungs that produce coughing, fever, and weakness. It may also attack the central nervous system in later stages. The fungus causing it is thought to infect after having been inhaled; it has been found in chicken and pigeon droppings.

Histoplasmosis (HIHS-toh-plaaz-MOH-sihs): Histoplasmosis is marked by lung infection but may spread to include ulceration of the digestive tract, skin lesions, and damage to vital organs. It results from inhalation of spores found in droppings, such as bat guano in a cave or bird droppings beneath a popular roosting spot. It is most dangerous for those with impaired immune systems.

Prevention of disabling fungus diseases: Cases of the more disabling fungus diseases occur with comparatively high frequency among persons with AIDS or with other immune system suppression conditions. Individuals with such cancers as lymphoma and leukemia also have a relatively high incidence of severe fungus diseases. Persons with advanced cases of diabetes mellitus seem especially susceptible to fungus diseases. For them these diseases may be held in check by maintaining otherwise good health and using tight control of blood sugar.

G

Gallstones

DISEASE

TYPE: CHEMICAL; MECHANICAL

The gallbladder is a pear-shaped reservoir that holds about a cup of a complex liquid called *bile,* which is produced by the liver. Crystals, called *gallstones* or just stones, settle out of bile from time to time. Small stones can grow in a gallbladder without causing any problems. But if a stone happens to get stuck in the small passage, or duct, that leads from the gallbladder to the intestines, sharp pains and potentially serious complications may follow.

On the Internet
NATIONAL DIGESTIVE DISEASES
INFORMATION CLEARINGHOUSE
digestive.niddk.nih.gov/
ddiseases/pubs/gallstones/

Cause: Bile, which flows from the liver into the gallbladder, is normally rich in cholesterol. It also contains bilirubin (BIHL-ih-ROO-bihn), a waste product formed when the liver breaks down old red blood cells. Either may form a small crystal in the gallbladder. Over time layers of material gradually enlarge the crystal until it becomes a gallstone. Stones can be small and sharp-edged or larger and smoother.

Doctors do not know exactly why some people develop gallstones and others do not. Diet, heredity, and hormonal influences have been identified as factors by different researchers. Medical researchers increasingly suspect that a diet high in cholesterol contributes to the formation of gallstones. Others have observed that women develop gallstones more often than men and have proposed that the female hormone estrogen causes changes in bile.

Stones in the gallbladder usually cause no problems, although they sometimes irritate the lining of the gallbladder, a condition called *chronic cholecystitis* (KOH-lih-sih-STIY-tihs). They sometimes pass harmlessly through the duct out of the gallbladder (the cystic duct) and into the bile duct that leads to the intestine. But if a stone gets stuck in the cystic duct and causes inflammation, an extremely painful condition called *acute cholecystitis* results. This pain is known as *biliary colic.* If the stone passes further and becomes stuck in the bile duct, there may be repeated episodes of biliary colic. A gallstone that remains stuck in the bile duct can lead to serious complications and requires immediate medical attention.

Incidence: An estimated 25 million Americans and 2 million Canadians have gallstones—nearly one person in ten. The condition leads to surgery in about 500,000 Americans a year, but fewer than 5,000 of them die from the disease.

Women have more than double the chance of developing gallstones as men, and incidence increases with age for both sexes at a rate that averages 1 to 3% per year. Native Americans are especially prone to gallstones; in Canada as many as 70 to 80% of Native Americans have gallstones. Also, certain diseases can be linked with gallstone formation, including diabetes mellitus and cystic fibrosis.

Although gallstones have been known since ancient times,

they have been on the increase in industrialized countries, where overeating tends to be more common. Also, the incidence of gallstones appears to increase in countries that are developing rapidly, especially where Western diet is becoming more popular.

Noticeable symptoms: When a gallstone gets stuck either in the cystic or bile duct, a person experiences intense pain in the upper abdomen (toward the right side and often radiating around to the back). Nausea and vomiting usually accompany the pain, which lasts for a few hours before finally subsiding. ***Go to an emergency room and obtain medical treatment immediately if these symptoms occur.***

Diagnosis: The first test is for the presence of a sharp pain when the physician presses below the rib cage and has the patient take a deep breath. This will likely be followed by a blood test for indications of elevated liver enzymes caused by bile backing up into the liver. One of several different tests based on x-rays or an ultrasound scan will determine if a stone has blocked a duct and the size and location of the stone.

Treatment options: Doctors have several different approaches to treating gallstones and the blockages they cause. The most common approach, which is nearly always successful, is surgery. Two nonsurgical treatments are also available.

Surgery can involve removing just a single stone blocking the bile duct or, in more serious cases, removing the gallbladder as well. The gallbladder is not an essential organ, and a person can live a normal life without one.

Most operations use a laparoscope, a small tube that transmits images of internal organs to a monitor in the operating room. The surgeon makes small "postage-stamp" incisions for inserting the laparoscope and other tubes that carry tiny instruments, such as microscissors. By watching the monitor while manipulating instruments from outside the patient, the surgeon performs the operation. When removing the gallbladder, the surgeon first uses the laparoscope to remove stones blocking the bile duct. Then the gallbladder is deflated by emptying it, and it is finally removed. The whole procedure takes less than an hour and eliminates any further problems with gallstones.

The same operation can be performed in the traditional

Emergency Room

High fiber

Exercise

way with a long incision in the patient's right side. This is a major operation, however, with potentially greater risk of complications, but it is preferred when the gallbladder is inflamed. About one in five operations requires the larger incision.

When a single small stone is involved, the doctor may recommend a nonsurgical procedure called *lithotripsy* (LITH-uh-TRIHP-see). Here the stone is pulverized by sending shock waves through the skin, clearing up the blockage immediately. This option is not available everywhere, since special equipment is required.

Drug therapy to dissolve gallstones is a rarely used nonsurgical option when a blockage is not involved. But drug therapy can take up to two years and works in only about half the cases. In half of cases of this type of nonsurgical removal new stones will form.

Prevention: People who tend to get gallstones should aim for a diet high in fiber and low in cholesterol and fats. Keeping weight at a healthy level and engaging in regular exercise are also important.

Gangrene

SYMPTOM

See also
Aneurysm
Circulatory system
Diabetes mellitus, type 1
Diabetes mellitus, type 2
Embolism
Frostbite
Hardening of the arteries
Tobacco and disease

Sometimes the blood supply necessary to keep tissue healthy is interrupted. The lack of blood can cause gangrene—the death of cells and decay of tissue. Toxins that kill cells, most often toxins released by bacteria, can also cause gangrene. Wounds contaminated by soil may develop gas gangrene, so called because bacteria release bubbles of gas that lodge in the dead flesh. Gas gangrene results from contamination by bacteria of the Clostridium family, best known for tetanus and botulism. Like its relatives, the bacterium that causes gas gangrene is common in soil and prefers a low-oxygen environment.

Parts affected: Gangrene can affect any part of the body. It is most common in the fingers or toes, hands or feet, or arms or legs. Gangrene is most dangerous, however, when it destroys internal organs.

Gangrene caused by loss of blood supply is usually limited to injured tissue. Gangrene caused by bacteria may spread to other parts of the body.

On the Internet
MAYO CLINIC
www.mayoclinic.com/health/
gangrene/HQ00737

Related symptoms: Gangrene often begins as localized fever and pain followed by numbness due to lack of circulation in the affected area. The skin turns black as tissue dies. Swelling, pus, and a foul smell are additional signs of gas gangrene.

Gangrene of internal organs may occur when an aneurysm ruptures, suddenly cutting off the blood supply, or when an organ becomes infected with bacteria from a wound or surgery. Gangrene of internal organs causes severe abdominal pain and a high temperature and can be fatal when vital organs are affected.

Associations: Blood vessels can be destroyed, crushed, or punctured by frostbite, burns, gunshot or stab wounds, or accidental injuries, making gangrene possible. In addition to a burst aneurysm, gangrene can occur in people who have an embolism or some other condition that involves poor blood circulation. Gangrene often affects the feet of people with diabetes mellitus. Gangrene occurs in people with *Buerger's disease,* also known as thromboangitis obliterans (THROM-buh-aan-JIY-tihs uh-BLIHT-uh-RAANZ), a circulatory system disorder that affects the fingers or toes, and that is primarily caused by smoking tobacco.

Relief of symptoms: People with injuries that may become gangrenous can take antibiotics to prevent or fight infection. If gangrene has already developed, surgery may be required to remove all dead tissue. Sometimes it is necessary to amputate a whole limb or part of a limb.

Prevention and possible actions: Make sure that burned or frostbitten skin is kept strictly clean at all times to avoid infection. *If an injured area feels very warm or painful, and skin begins to turn dark, or a wound smells bad, see a physician immediately.* People with diabetes should follow their treatment programs faithfully and take special care of their toes and feet.

Emergency Room

Gastritis

(gaa-STRIY-tihs)

SYMPTOM

Almost everyone experiences an occasional attack of gastritis, or stomach inflammation. Most mild cases of gastritis are short-lived and cause no lasting harm. But sometimes gastritis signals a serious problem.

On the Internet
INTELIHEALTH
www.intelihealth.com/IH/
ihtIH?t=10054

Phone doctor

Emergency Room

Avoid alcohol

No food

Avoid aspirin

Part affected: Gastritis is an inflammation of the mucous membrane that lines the stomach. Sores called lesions or raw areas may develop in the membrane; in this case the symptom is termed *erosive gastritis*. The affected areas may bleed, and there may be blood in vomit or stools.

Cause: *Acute gastritis* can be caused by the ingestion of an irritating substance, such as aspirin or ibuprofen, potassium or iron supplements, tobacco smoke, or too much food or alcohol. It can also result from a bacterial or viral infection or from stress, especially stress caused by a wound or burn. *Chronic gastritis* is an inflammation that occurs repeatedly or continually over a period of time; it is typically caused by a persistent disease. *Toxic gastritis* results from the ingestion of a corrosive substance such as a poison or an acid.

Associations: The most common diseases associated with chronic gastritis include alcoholism, food allergies, Crohn's disease, and hiatus hernia. The same bacterium that causes stomach ulcers also produces erosive gastritis in milder cases. Gastritis is one of the indications for cancer of the stomach. Pernicious anemia is often the outcome of an autoimmune disease that interferes with the stomach lining; in this case gastritis is the cause of the disease, since stomach inflammation prevents absorption of vitamin B_{12}.

Prevention and possible actions: Many cases of mild gastritis can be avoided by good dietary habits. See a doctor if you have severe or chronic gastritis. ***Toxic gastritis requires immediate medical attention.***

To control mild gastritis, a doctor may prescribe an antacid or bismuth subsalicylate (Pepto-Bismol). If the problem is caused by a drug, a change in medication may be recommended, or the doctor may suggest that you take the drug with food rather than between meals. Treatment of more severe gastritis will depend on the underlying cause. For example, erosive gastritis caused by the bacterium *Helicobacter pylori* can be treated with antibiotics.

Relief of symptoms: Do not eat and do not consume alcohol while you are nauseous or vomiting. When the symptoms subside, drink small amounts of water or weak tea at frequent intervals. After 24 hours begin to eat solid foods, taking only bland foods for at least a day or two. Aspirin or ibuprofen must be avoided, but acetaminophen is not harmful to the stomach lining.

Gastroenteritis

(GAAS-troh-EHN-tuh-RIY-tihs)

DISEASE

TYPE: INFECTIOUS (VARIOUS ORGANISMS); CHEMICAL

Rest

Drink water

Avoid alcohol

"Stomach flu," a "24-hour bug," "traveler's diarrhea," and "something I ate" refer to gastroenteritis, any infection or inflammation of the entire digestive tract.

Cause: Gastroenteritis is most commonly caused by viruses or bacteria, although protozoa, funguses, and worms may also be responsible. Sometimes food poisoning—caused by ingestion of bacteria, viruses, or toxic chemicals—results in gastroenteritis. Noroviruses (such as Norwalk virus) are the suspected cause of many cases of gastroenteritis among cruise ship passengers; these viruses are spread by consuming contaminated food, touching contaminated objects, or by direct contact with infected persons.

Noticeable symptoms: Nausea, vomiting, diarrhea, and fever are typical symptoms of gastroenteritis. Fatigue and muscle aches may occur, and the abdomen may be distended and tender. If the gastroenteritis does not clear up in several days, or if symptoms are severe, seek medical help.

Diagnosis: A white blood cell count can help indicate the presence of an infection. If the doctor suspects a serious infection, a stool culture may identify the exact cause.

Treatment options: A viral illness is left to run its course. Bed rest, liquids, such as water or weak tea, to replace lost fluids, and a bland diet all help. Avoid alcohol.

If the gastroenteritis requires medical attention, the doctor may prescribe medicines to relieve symptoms. If symptoms have caused dehydration, you may be hospitalized during intravenous infusion of fluids. When a specific organism has been identified, an appropriate medicine, such as an antibiot-

On the Internet
MEDLINE PLUS
www.nlm.nih.gov/medlineplus/
gastroenteritis.html

ic, will be prescribed. If the stomach is rejecting everything put into it, medicine may be administered intravenously or as a suppository.

Prevention: Traveler's diarrhea is usually bacterial gastroenteritis. Avoiding local water or the exterior portions of fresh fruits and vegetables is the main precaution one can take. Most viral gastroenteritis can also be spread in contaminated water and can even be contracted by swimming in water polluted with human waste. Another source can be shellfish that live in such water. But viral gastroenteritis can also spread on surfaces, such as silverware or utensils that have been handled by someone who has failed to wash thoroughly after defecation. It is a good idea to avoid eating anywhere that seems even slightly less than perfectly clean. Also, children in day care spread the disease to each other and to their parents; risks can be reduced if both children and parents wash their hands after playing with other children or their toys.

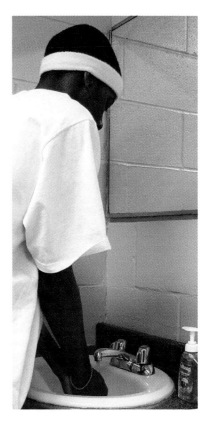

Nearly all gastroenteritis spreads by what is termed "the fecal-oral route"; that is, by human waste products that are carried to the mouth either on food or simply by dirty hands. Thorough washing of hands with soap and water after using the bathroom removes the main agent carrying disease by this route. One authority suggests that you sing all of "Happy Birthday to You" through twice while you wash to make sure that you are doing a thorough job.

Genetic diseases

On the Internet
HUMAN GENOME PROJECT
INFORMATION
www.ornl.gov/sci/techresources/
Human_Genome/medicine/
assist.shtml

Although DNA is designed to create exact copies of itself when a cell divides to produce two daughter cells, there are often errors in copying. A gene may be copied into the wrong part of a DNA molecule, part of the gene may fail to be copied, one part may be copied more than once, or a different base may be substituted for the original one (see Genome for further details). The cell has mechanisms to correct mistakes in copying or damage to the original DNA, but these mechanisms can also make mistakes. Changes caused by damage or copying errors, which are called mutations, may happen at any time. However, they have the greatest effect when they occur in a sperm or egg cell, for then the mutation is copied to all the other cells of a developing individual. In most cases, the mutation is harmful. If the mutation allows the human to survive to birth, the infant is born with a genetic disease. Rarely, a mutation results in a trait that is an evolutionary advantage instead of a genetic disease.

Dominant and recessive diseases: Genes work in pairs. With few exceptions, each gene from your father has a corresponding gene from your mother, and they interact to determine the traits that are expressed in you. A child inherits half the genes of each parent—one gene of each pair from the father, and one of each pair from the mother. Which gene of a pair the child inherits is a matter of chance.

If both genes in the pair are the same (and most gene pairs are identical), they simply reinforce each other. But if they differ in any significant way, the resulting trait may be a blend of the effects of each gene. Or one of the genes, called the dominant gene, may produce a noticeable trait, overcoming the recessive gene.

Genes are portions of the DNA molecules found in every cell. The genes, singly or in combination with other genes or influences from the environment, determine what cells produce and how they behave. As a human develops from a fertilized egg, almost all physical (and many mental) characteristics are genetic traits. Instructions for these traits are transmitted in the form of genes, half from the father and half from the mother; the genes were brought together when the father's sperm fertilized the mother's egg. If the traits produced during development interfere with normal physical or mental functioning, the disorder is called a genetic disease.

A dominant genetic disease can be inherited directly from one parent who has the abnormal gene and thus also has the disease. But a recessive disease must be inherited from both parents, and they may not be affected themselves. Instead, they may be carriers, each of whom has a matched pair containing one normal, dominant gene and one abnormal, recessive gene. Not only are carriers not affected, they may not even know that they possess the abnormal gene.

The chances of whether a child will inherit a genetic disease also depend upon whether the disease is dominant or recessive. The child of a parent with an abnormal dominant gene has a one-in-two chance of inheriting the abnormal gene, and the same one-in-two chance of inheriting the other, normal gene from the affected parent's pair. Even though the other, unaffected parent has two normal genes, the risk of the child inheriting the abnormal gene, and of having the disease, remains one in two.

The child of parents who are carriers of abnormal recessive genes has a one-in-four chance of inheriting normal genes from both parents, a two-in-four chance of inheriting one normal and one abnormal gene (and of being a carrier like the parents), and a one-in-four chance of inheriting abnormal genes from both parents (and of having the genetic disease).

The best-known dominant genetic disease is probably Huntington's disease. Well-known recessive diseases include cystic fibrosis, sickle-cell anemia, and Tay-Sachs disease. *Gaucher* (GOH-shay) *disease* is a relatively common recessive disease caused by one of several mutations on chromosome 1. Each defect prevents cells from breaking down a particular fatlike chemical, which then accumulates and interferes with cell functions. Treatment consists of replacing the defective enzyme with a functioning one.

X-linked diseases: Another type of genetic disease is called X-linked, because the abnormal genes are transmitted in the X chromosome. The best-known X-linked diseases are hemophilia and muscular dystrophy. They affect boys almost exclusively because X-linked diseases have a very different pattern of inheritance.

Genes are not passed on to offspring individually, but in the form of long strings called chromosomes, each containing a double-stranded molecule of DNA. Each child receives a set of 23 chromosomes from the mother, mostly matched to 23 from the father. The 23rd pair, however, determines sex and may not match. This can be composed of two large chromosomes known as X, or of one X chromosome and a much smaller Y chromosome. Children who inherit two X chromosomes develop as girls, while those with an X and a Y develop into boys. A girl inherits one X chromosome from her mother and one from her father, but a boy derives the Y from his father.

The large X chromosomes contain many genes, but the Y chromosome is much smaller and contains very few genes. Therefore, a boy develops many traits from the single X chromosome he receives from his mother. Thus, a boy may inherit a genetic disease from a defective gene in his mother's X chromosome. A girl, inheriting the same defective gene from her mother but a normal gene from her father, may be unaffected. But this girl is nonetheless a carrier, with a one-in-two chance of passing the abnormal gene to her children. And each of her male children has a one-in-two chance of having an X-linked disease caused by the abnormal gene.

Familial diseases and chromosomal abnormalities: Some genetic diseases result from interactions between more than one pair of genes or between genes and environmental factors. Such diseases are called familial. They run in families, but their pattern of inheritance is not clear. Examples include familial hypercholesterolemia and neural tube defects. Certain disorders that are sometimes described as genetic are not caused by abnormal genes, but by defects in whole chromosomes. These disorders are discussed at the entry Chromosomal abnormalities.

Incidence: The number of known genetic diseases is larger than that of either infectious or autoimmune diseases. There are from 20,000 to 25,000 different gene pairs in each human being, which allows many opportunities for harmful mutations. Moreover, many genes can be mutated in more than one way, some ways producing different outcomes, mostly harmful but a few beneficial.

Many harmful mutations produce results that are not plainly observable. For example, they may prevent a fertilized egg from developing, so that no pregnancy results, or have such serious effects that the fetus is spontaneously aborted during very early pregnancy. One estimate is that every human being carries from three to five recessive genes that would be harmful to health if expressed. Estimates vary widely on how many genetic diseases occur in humans. A recent survey found more than 6,000 identifiable genetic diseases and many more familial diseases.

A Canadian study of more than a million live births revealed about 3.6 in 1,000 had disorders caused by single genes. Nearly half of these were caused by recessive genes, less than one-seventh were X-linked, and the remainder were caused by dominant genes. Combinations of genetic defects that are thought to be the basis of familial diseases resulted in diseases in 46.4 of 1,000 persons who were followed from birth to the age of 25. The study also found 1.2 in 1,000 births resulted in genetic disorders that the scientists could not classify as to origin. When all diseases with a genetic component of any kind were combined, the total reached 53 in 1,000 live births.

Several factors affect the incidence of particular genetic diseases. Some diseases are concentrated in specific ethnic groups. Gaucher's and Tay-Sachs diseases, for example, are part of a group of genetic diseases that occur most often in Ashkenazic Jews from eastern Europe. Also, if the mother and father are related to each other, they share many of the same genes, raising the risk of a recessive disorder in their children.

Detection of abnormal genes: Many abnormal genes can be identified in cells of individuals who have them, including cells of fetuses. Tests are now available for nearly 1,000 genetic diseases.

- Some defects can be identified by gene products: Chemical analysis reveals that the protein a gene normally produces is absent, deficient, or abnormal. For example, carriers of the gene for Tay-Sachs disease, as well as offspring who have the disease, can be identified by this method.
- Other genetic diseases can be identified by DNA analysis: Specific genes along the long, chainlike molecule of DNA are isolated and analyzed. People who have the gene for Huntington's disease can be identified by this technique, long before any symptoms appear. So can most carriers of the gene for cystic fibrosis.

The number of genetic diseases that can be diagnosed by such methods is constantly increasing.

Genetic engineering

REFERENCE

See also
Genetic diseases
Genome
Growth
Vaccination and disease

On the Internet
GEENOR
www.geneticengineering.org/

Genetic engineering is any artificial change in a gene that causes cells to produce a different product. Sometimes this involves insertion of genes from one species into a different species.

How it is done: In bacteria small rings of DNA are easily transferred from one bacterium to another, even to members of another species. Scientists can splice a new gene into a ring and insert the altered ring into another bacterium, where the new gene produces its product. Different techniques are used to genetically engineer animal or plant cells. Scientists may add a new gene to a virus, which transfers the gene when it infects a cell. Or genes on tiny pellets are shot into the nucleus of a cell. In either case, the location of the new gene is random, and usually the gene does not function properly. But when the gene is put into many cells at once, scientists can select those cells that exhibit signs that the gene is working. The few cells with a successful gene transfer are then cultured to produce numerous daughter cells.

Genetically engineered medicines: One of the earliest examples of genetic engineering was insertion of the human gene for insulin production into bacteria in 1980. Insulin produced by bacteria is less expensive than insulin derived from nonhuman animal sources and sometimes more effective. Today the most commonly used products of genetic engineering include the virus-fighting interferons; human growth hormone; t-PA (tissue plasminogen activator), used to break up blood clots; erythropoietin (EPO), a growth factor for red blood cells; and various vaccines, notably for hepatitis B. Many of these substances are produced by genes inserted into animal cells.

Genetically engineered foods: Genetic engineering has also been used to change the genomes of plants, a procedure that has proved to be controversial. Crops such as corn have had bacterial genes inserted to provide pest resistance or faster growth. Fruits have been given plant genes that provide better preservative qualities.

Some persons object to genetically engineered foods. They believe that foreign genes might spread to wild plants through natural reproduction (such as pollen from genetically engineered plants fertilizing wild ones) and that food from genetically engineered sources might contain harmful chemicals. Studies so far show only a slight chance of the escape of artificial genes to a wild population and no evidence of danger to the food supply.

Genital herpes

DISEASE

TYPE: INFECTIOUS (VIRAL)

See also
Birth canal
Cancers
Chicken pox
Cold sore
Shingles
STD (sexually transmitted diseases)
Viruses and disease

On the Internet
NATIONAL INSTITUTE
OF ALLERGY AND INFECTIOUS
DISEASES
www.niaid.nih.gov/factsheets/
stdherp.htm

Did You Know?

It is a myth that you can get genital herpes from a toilet seat. The virus is weakened when exposed to air, and there are no proven cases of someone getting the disease from a toilet seat.

In the 1970s, before anyone had heard of AIDS, a sexually transmitted disease that had suddenly become epidemic caused many people to change their sexual practices. The infection, commonly called "herpes" but more specifically genital herpes, usually continued for life. Today it is estimated that 86 million people worldwide are infected with the disease.

Women infected with genital herpes had special concerns. Genital herpes is thought to contribute to cervical cancer. In addition, when women infected with herpes have children, the babies may need to be delivered by cesarean section to prevent infection of the newborn. A baby may be severely affected if the mother has an outbreak near delivery.

Cause: Infection with herpes simplex virus type 2 (HSV-2) causes genital herpes. HSV-2 is one of a closely related family, the herpesviruses, including the herpes simplex virus type 1 (HSV-1), which causes cold sores; the *Varicella* virus of chicken pox and shingles; the *Epstein-Barr virus,* which causes mononucleosis; and *cytomegalovirus* (SIY-tuh-MEHG-uh-loh-VIY-ruhs), which normally causes a mild infection but may be a serious disease in patients with a weakened immune system.

Incidence: An estimated 25% of the U.S. population over the age of 12 is infected with HSV-2. Public health experts estimate that more than half of those infected do not have symptoms and do not know that they are infected. There are nearly 600,000 new infections each year in the United States and Canada.

Noticeable symptoms: Small water-filled blisters appear at the site of infection on the genitals. Flulike symptoms, such as fever and swollen lymph nodes, often accompany the initial outbreak. The blisters are similar to the cold sores caused by HSV-1.

Diagnosis: Since other diseases cause similar symptoms, it is important to see a physician when the first symptoms appear so that an accurate diagnosis can be made. If sores are visible, fluid from them can be tested for antibodies to the virus.

Treatment options: Genital herpes cannot be cured, but medications can relieve pain and itching. A physician may also suggest procedures to reduce discomfort, such as applying ice packs, wearing loose clothing, and keeping the genitals dry.

Prescription antiviral medications, such as acyclovir, can reduce the frequency of occurrence of symptoms and reduce the intensity when symptoms do reappear.

Stages and progress: The virus is transmitted during sex acts when there is contact with the mucous membranes of the penis, vagina, mouth, or anus. A few days to a few weeks after infection, blisters filled with water form at the site of infection. Blisters may also form on the groin and buttocks. The area may itch and be painful. The blisters fill with pus and break open, forming raw, red sores. The sores heal in several weeks. The newly infected person may also have headaches, swollen lymph nodes near the point of infection, fever, vaginal discharge, general fatigue, and muscle soreness. When an episode of infection runs its course, the virus retreats to nerve cells near the base of the spine and becomes dormant.

The first episode of HSV-2 is usually the worst. During this initial attack the immune system produces antibodies that help fight future outbreaks. Some individuals have only a single episode during which blisters appear. But many people infected with HSV-2 have repeated outbreaks, sometimes as many as 6 to 12 during a year. Usually, outbreaks become less frequent and less severe over time. It is during outbreaks that the infected person is most likely to transmit HSV-2 to a sexual partner.

During an outbreak personal hygiene is very important. HSV-2 is so infectious that touching an open herpes sore, then touching another part of the body, can spread the virus. It is important to avoid scratching the blisters. Scratching can spread the infection and leave the blistered area open to other infections. Personal items, such as towels, washcloths, and clothing, should not be shared during this period.

Prevention and risk factors: The best approach to HSV-2 is avoidance. ***Do not have sex with anyone who has sores on his or her genitals.*** This is fairly easy to observe with men, but with women the sores may be deep in the vagina and not visible. Using a condom can help, but this is not foolproof since the herpes blisters may occur beyond the area protected by a condom.

Genome

(JEE-nohm)

On the Internet

HUMAN GENOME PROJECT
INFORMATION
www.ornl.gov/sci/techresources/
Human_Genome/home.shtml

During the past 100 years major breakthroughs have expanded our understanding of how inherited, or genetic, information orchestrates all of the body's functions. Scientists learned that individual hereditary units exist, units that came to be called *genes,* and that these are segments of strands of the chemical deoxyribonucleic (dee-OK-see-RIY-boh-noo-KLEE-ihk) acid, or DNA. DNA provides a library of instructions that directs the body's development and functions by making thousands of different proteins. Proteins not only make up significant parts of the body tissues but also, as enzymes and hormones, control all body processes. The totality of DNA in an individual is called the genome—this includes the genes and parts of DNA that do not act as genes. The body is not completely determined by the genome, however, as nutrition, experience, and other factors interact with the genome throughout development.

Size and location: Each strand of DNA is a long molecule made up of building blocks called bases. These are lined up like beads in a necklace. Each base consists of phosphorus, sugar, and one of four nucleotides (NOO-klee-uh-TIYDZ): adenine (AAD-n-een) (A), thymine (THIY-meen) (T), guanine (GWAY-neen) (G), and cytosine (SIY-tuh-seen) (C). Normally, DNA occurs as a coiled double strand. When uncoiled, it looks like a ladder whose rungs are formed by pairs of nucleotides, one from each strand. The two nucleotides in each rung are held together by weak chemical bonds.

One molecule of DNA is the working part of a tiny structure called a *chromosome.* The 23 pairs of human chromosomes are crowded together as tangled strands within a cell's nucleus, a region only a few micrometers across. But if you took all the DNA from one cell nucleus and laid it end to end, it would stretch more than a meter. The chromosomes are made up of DNA and proteins that aid DNA in its activities. Every human cell contains a nucleus that includes the chromosomes, although eggs and sperm cells have only half the number of chromosomes as other cells. Some of the DNA in the genome is not in the nucleus but in small bodies in cells called mitochondria (MIY-tuh-KON-dree-uh); there it directs production of energy for the cell.

The Human Genome Project has been mapping the location of all the genes. It now appears that there are approximately 20,000 to 25,000 different genes in each human, although the same gene may vary somewhat between people or even between paired chromosomes in the same person. Each different version of a gene is called an *allele* (uh-LEEL).

Role: A sequence of three nucleotides in DNA forms a "word" in the genetic code. Most of the words indicate one of the 20 different amino acids. For example, guanine-cytosine-adenine, or GCA, is one of four codes for the amino acid alanine. A sequence of genetic code words forms the instructions for creating a sequence of amino acids, which link together to form a protein. Other code words give directions like "start" and "stop." DNA stays in a cell's nucleus, but proteins are assembled outside the nucleus from amino acids floating in the cytoplasm.

A person's genome directs every biological activity in life. At conception the genome begins to direct the cell division, growth, and development of the embryo. In the early stages of development all of the genetic information is available in all of the cells. But as development goes on, and some cells become specialized as bone, others as muscle, and still others as brain cells, some of the genes in each cell are turned off. No genetic information is lost; it is just that the information that is not needed becomes unavailable in that particular type of cell.

The specific combination of alleles in the genome of an individual is known as his or her genotype (JEHN-uh-TIYP). For example, the specific gene for blue eyes can be a part of a person's genotype, while the general genes for eye color (there are at least three) are part of the genome.

The genotype does not by itself determine the traits of the adult organism. The traits that appear, or are *expressed*, taken together, are called the phenotype (FEE-nuh-TIYP). Which traits from the genotype are expressed may be affected by the environment. For example, a person with the genotype for blue eyes can have the eyes turn brown by using a glaucoma medicine called latanoprost.

The role of RNA: Although the genome consists of DNA, all the operations of DNA are carried out by a closely related molecule called ribonucleic (RIY-boh-noo-KLEE-ihk) acid, or RNA.

The main differences between DNA and RNA are that RNA is single stranded, and instead of the base thymine, it has a base named uracil (YOOR-uh-sihl). RNA copies the base sequence from a gene and transfers it to another RNA molecule in a part of the cell called a ribosome (RIY-buh-sohm). Another form of RNA brings the building blocks of proteins to the ribosome, where the RNA assembles the ingredients into the protein specified by the gene. The protein, by interacting with other proteins, carries out the expression of the original gene. For example, it could be a protein that influences eye color.

Some viruses have "genomes" that consist of RNA instead of DNA. These viruses include those responsible for poliomyelitis, influenza, and AIDS. Some scientists believe that RNA also plays a role in the development of certain genetic diseases that are caused by repeats of single or small groups of nucleotides in DNA—diseases that include fragile X syndrome and Huntington's disease. Other rare genetic diseases are caused by errors in the way RNA works in building proteins, although the errors can also be traced back to a defect in a gene.

In recent years scientists have discovered a form of RNA that can be used to make a specific gene stop producing its product —the gene is silenced. This is called RNAi for "RNA interference." It is already an important research tool, and there is hope that in the future RNAi can be used to treat some genetic diseases by silencing a gene that produces a harmful protein.

Conditions that affect the genome: Many things in the environment can damage DNA—including viruses, pollution, radiation, poisons, and sunlight. Damaged genes may quit producing needed proteins. Cell mechanisms regularly repair minor damage, but if injury is widespread, it can cause severe illness or even death.

High-energy radiation, from ultraviolet light to gamma rays or from radioactivity, can damage the genome or parts of it. For example, high doses of radioactivity can destroy the body's ability to create new blood cells. When this happens, death usually follows. Smaller amounts of radiation can cause cells to revert to a less specialized state and cause them to begin dividing rapidly. This rapid, uncontrolled cell division is called cancer.

All viruses use part of the genome to help themselves reproduce. In the case of *HIV infection* the virus tricks the cell into using its genetic instructions instead of those of the white blood cell's DNA. The DNA in a cell infected with HIV becomes a factory for making more HIV rather than all of the other proteins needed by the cell to survive. When enough white blood cells are destroyed, the victim dies.

When harm to the genome occurs in body cells, it affects only the person whose cells are damaged. But if the damage happens to the genetic material in the cells that produce eggs and sperm, it can be passed on to the offspring of the affected person. These changes, or mutations, are the origin of genetic diseases.

GERD (gastroesophageal reflux disease)

(GAAS-troh-ih-SOF-uh-JEE-uhl)

DISEASE

TYPE: MECHANICAL

See also
Chest pain
Diaphragm
Digestive system
Esophagus
Gastritis
Heartburn
Hernias
Stomach

On the Internet
ASTRAZENECA
www.gerd.com/

Most people experience an occasional bout of heartburn—the painful burning sensation under the breastbone caused when stomach acid rises into the esophagus. But for some it happens so frequently that it is considered gastroesophageal reflux disease, or GERD.

Cause: The place where the esophagus and stomach meet is a complex set of muscles called a sphincter (SFINGK-tuhr). When we swallow, the sphincter opens, allowing food into the stomach. Then the sphincter closes, keeping the stomach contents from backing up into the esophagus. Stomach contents contain acid that is necessary for digestion. The lining of the stomach is protected from this acid, but the lining of the esophagus is not. When there is frequent, severe backup, or *reflux,* of acid stomach contents into the esophagus, a person is said to have GERD.

The cause of GERD probably varies. GERD may be related to weakening of the sphincter at the base of the esophagus. Another theory is that GERD is related to hiatus hernia. The esophagus passes through the diaphragm, a large muscle that separates the chest from the abdomen, to reach the stomach. If this opening (hiatus) enlarges, the top of the stomach may push up into the chest and make it easier for the stomach contents to back up into the esophagus. Overeating, smoking, alcohol, overweight, certain postures, and being pregnant can also contribute to acid reflux into the esophagus.

Incidence: An estimated 130 million Americans experience heartburn once a month. Thirty million have GERD symptoms daily. GERD is most common in people over 50, but can occur at any age. It has even been diagnosed in infants and young children. In this age group it often shows up as frequent vomiting; many children outgrow GERD as they grow older.

Noticeable symptoms: Both frequent heartburn and a burning acid taste in the back of the mouth that happens frequently and cannot be controlled by antacids, separately or together, may be signs of GERD. These symptoms may be especially severe when lying down or bending over after eating. Coughing and a persistent sore throat may occur as well.

Diagnosis: If the symptoms cannot be controlled by antacids or by medications the doctor prescribes, the physician can do an examination of the esophagus and stomach. The patient swallows a tube called an endoscope that allows the doctor to look at the inside of the esophagus. In severe cases of GERD there are breaks, or ulcers, in the lining of the esophagus. In some cases a condition called *Barrett's esophagus* occurs where the lining of the esophagus changes and becomes more like the lining of the stomach. Barrett's esophagus is considered quite serious because it can lead to cancer.

Treatment: Most cases of GERD can be treated with prescription medications and lifestyle changes. The patient may be asked to keep a journal to try to identify events or foods that trigger an attack. Alcohol and smoking nearly always contribute to making the disease worse. Quite a few medications, ranging from aspirin to birth control pills, can also contribute.

One common remedy is lifting the head of the bed by at least 6 inches by putting blocks under the bed's legs at the head end.

Over-the-counter drugs ranging from antacids to medicines such as Tagamet HB or Zantac 75 designed to lower production of stomach acid are helpful in mild cases, but most persons with GERD need stronger prescription drugs.

Surgery is an option to tighten the sphincter. If Barrett's esophagus develops, surgery may be necessary to prevent cancer from developing.

Avoid alcohol

Don't smoke

Avoid aspirin

Giardia

(jee-AHR-dee-uh)

DISEASE

TYPE: INFECTIOUS
(PARASITICAL)

See also
Animal diseases and humans
Cryptosporidiosis
Diarrhea
Dysentery
Gastroenteritis
Parasites and disease

On the Internet
CENTERS FOR DISEASE CONTROL
AND PREVENTION (CDC)
www.cdc.gov/ncidod/dpd/
parasites/giardiasis/
factsht_giardia.htm

"Beaver fever," or *giardiasis* (JEE-ahr-DIY-uh-sihs), is familiarly known as giardia to campers and hikers. The disease has long-lasting diarrhea as the main symptom.

Cause: Giardiasis is caused by a microscopic, one-cell protozoan, *Giardia lamblia*. The dormant stage of this intestinal parasite, called giardia cysts, are passed out of the body of an infected human or animal in feces, where they can contaminate lakes, rivers, and ponds. When a suitable host ingests the cysts, they activate in the intestines, and the parasites feed and reproduce. Cysts can also be passed from an infected person to an uninfected person when the infected person does not wash properly after using the bathroom.

Outbreaks of the disease can result from drinking contaminated water or using it to wash food that is eaten raw. Irrigating produce with contaminated water and poor hygiene in daycare centers and facilities for the ill, disabled, or elderly also have been linked to outbreaks.

Incidence: Giardia is the most common nonbacterial cause of diarrhea in North America. More than 55,000 Americans and Canadians are newly infected each year. Giardiasis is even more prevalent worldwide; as many as one person in five is infected at any given time in developing countries.

Noticeable symptoms: Some individuals with giardia show no symptoms at all. Most have diarrhea that lasts from a few weeks to a few months. Rapid weight loss is noticeable. Those afflicted may experience cramps, fatigue, and nausea as well.

Diagnosis: A physician will determine if there has been exposure to a known source of the parasite and also take a smear of a stool sample to see if parasites or their cysts are present.

Treatment options: Some people get well naturally. Others are helped by antiparasite medication.

Stages and progress: Taking in fewer than ten giardia cysts can result in infection. As the parasite reproduces and begins to live in the intestines, the body becomes less efficient in absorbing food and water. Diarrhea and weight loss occur. These symptoms usually appear within two to three weeks of infection. In most

No matter how clean and clear water from a stream may appear, it is not safe to drink it unless it has been boiled or otherwise treated to kill parasites.

people the disease runs its course in a few weeks to a few months. But in some people it becomes chronic. People with HIV infection or another immune system problem may not be able to get the parasite out of their bodies, even with the help of medicine.

There is some evidence that having giardiasis once and getting over it provides immunity to future infection. For this reason giardia infection is more common in children than in adults.

Prevention: The risk of infection can be reduced by using bottled water or by boiling water when camping or traveling where water quality may be questionable. Good personal hygiene is an important preventive measure. Thorough hand washing after using the bathroom, after changing a diaper, and after playing with a cat or dog with diarrhea reduces the risk of becoming infected with giardia and other intestinal parasites.

Boil water

Wash hands

Gingivitis

(JIHN-juh-VIY-tihs)

Gingivitis is the formal name for *gum inflammation,* describing gums that are red and swollen and that bleed easily. Gingivitis may be accompanied by soreness and tenderness, but sometimes there is no noticeable discomfort.

Cause and associations: By far the most common cause of gingivitis is exposure to bacteria in plaque, the sticky film that forms naturally on teeth. The bacteria release toxins, substances that can irritate or damage the surrounding soft tis-

Flossing your teeth

Brushing cannot reach all tooth surfaces. Plaque and tartar tend to build up between the teeth, leading to both decay and gingivitis. Floss every time you brush your teeth. Draw the floss up and down, not just back and forth, between each pair of teeth so as to dislodge the plaque accumulating there.

See also

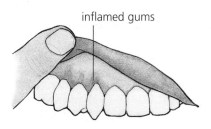

inflamed gums

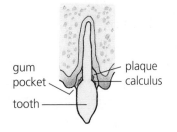

gum pocket
tooth
plaque
calculus

Calculus cannot be removed by brushing, but only by periodic professional cleaning, scraping, and polishing.

sues. Moreover, plaque soon hardens into calculus, or tartar, which is itself irritating and also harbors bacteria.

The gums may suffer from mechanical irritation caused by brushing the teeth too hard, eating hot or rough food (pizza mouth), or getting food fragments caught between teeth and gums. Another common cause is infection of the gums themselves by bacteria (canker sores, trench mouth), viruses (cold sores), or funguses (candidiasis). Gingivitis is especially common during pregnancy, when the levels of female hormones greatly increase. It can also be triggered by hormonal changes during puberty and by hormones in birth control pills. Gingivitis also may accompany such diseases as diabetes mellitus, lupus (systemic lupus erythematosus), and hypothyroidism.

Gingivitis may be an early symptom of periodontal disease, which can permanently damage the gums and tooth sockets. It is also a major symptom of two uncommon degenerative diseases of the gums and jaws: *desquamative* (dehs-KWAH-muh-tihv) *gingivitis,* which occurs mainly among older women, and *periodontosis* (PEHR-ee-uh-don-TOH-sihs), which mainly affects teenagers.

Prevention and treatment: The best way to prevent gingivitis and to treat its underlying causes is to remove plaque by daily brushing and flossing and to remove calculus by periodic professional cleaning. Brushing and flossing before going to bed are especially important. Using toothpastes and mouthwashes designed to reduce plaque and tartar may be helpful as well. Avoiding tobacco lowers the risk of gingivitis and speeds recovery from it.

Rinsing the mouth with warm saltwater or applying ice or a paste of baking soda to the sore areas may be soothing. Over-the-counter topical anesthetics—*topical* means that they are applied directly to the gums—can give temporary relief. Do not use antibiotics or steroidal ointments, such as hydrocortisone, unless they have been prescribed by your doctor or dentist.

Glaucoma

(glaw-KOH-muh)

DISEASE

TYPE: MECHANICAL

See also
Diabetes mellitus, type 1
Diabetes mellitus, type 2
Eyes and vision

On the Internet
GLAUCOMA RESEARCH
FOUNDATION
www.glaucoma.org/learn/

> **Did You Know?**
> A recent survey shows that fewer than half of all adult Americans are getting regular dilated eye exams, which are the best and most effective way to detect glaucoma.

Emergency Room

Glaucoma is a group of diseases of the eye that, if left untreated, can lead to progressive loss of sight in one or both eyes. Most common are chronic forms that develop slowly. Acute forms, which erupt in a sudden, violent attack, also occur.

Cause: In a normal eye, a fluid called the *aqueous* (AY-kwee-uhs) *humor* constantly flows through a small chamber at the front of the eyeball, bathing the lens and iris. Excess fluid drains out of the eye into the bloodstream. Glaucoma begins when optic nerves start to degenerate. Drainage outlets become blocked, causing fluid pressure to build within the eye. The aqueous humor presses on the larger vitreous cavity behind the lens. The compressed tissues eventually die, and sight in the affected eye is progressively damaged.

Glaucoma can also be caused by disease or injury to the eye, or occur at birth as a congenital condition.

Incidence: Incidence estimates are difficult to determine because it is believed that 50% or more of people with glaucoma are unaware of their disease. Worldwide about 65 million people are believed to be affected, with about 10% of them suffering from blindness in both eyes. In the United States about 2.2 million people have glaucoma. African Americans are three times more likely than Caucasian Americans to have the disease.

Noticeable symptoms: Chronic glaucoma develops so gradually that a person may not be aware of it until a substantial amount of damage has occurred. The first symptom is a loss of peripheral (side) vision, but in time central fine-focus vision will also decrease. In advanced stages, a glaucoma victim is likely to see the world in hazy, color-diminished tones.

A person suffering an attack of acute glaucoma may see halos around lights, but usually onset is dramatic and painful. The eye becomes hard and red, parts of the visual field suddenly disappear, and the person may have nausea and vomiting. *Acute glaucoma should be treated as a medical emergency.*

Diagnosis: As part of a regular eye examination, the ophthalmologist measures the pressure within the eye. The device used is a *tonometer* (toh-NOM-uh-tuhr), an instrument that

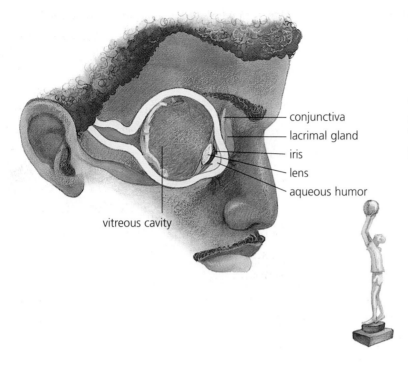

conjunctiva
lacrimal gland
iris
lens
aqueous humor

vitreous cavity

Glaucoma is a serious eye condition caused by blocked drainage channels. These result in damaging high pressure inside the eyeball.

measures pressure exerted by the aqueous fluid. The physician also tests the patient's peripheral vision. The examiner also checks the optic nerve at the back of the eye using a type of illuminated microscope called a *slit lamp.*

Treatment options: Treatment for glaucoma is designed to slow progression of the disease so that as much vision as possible is retained. Any vision already lost is gone forever. Types of treatment available include medications and surgery.

Several drugs are available to control chronic glaucoma. They are chiefly administered as eye drops, and a patient should expect to take the medications for life. ***Glaucoma medications are potent drugs. Never take them without food or in combination with other medications without consulting a physician.***

Laser surgery may be used in early stages of chronic glaucoma as a means of forestalling the use of glaucoma drugs. The surgery creates an artificial opening in the affected eye through which the aqueous humor can drain. If medication and laser treatments do not reduce pressure within the eye, a surgeon may need to create an open incision in the wall of the eye to drain some of the aqueous humor.

Some cases of glaucoma, called secondary glaucoma, are caused by other diseases or by drugs such as corticosteroids. In these cases, the underlying cause must be treated. Congenital glaucoma, present at birth, is corrected surgically.

Prevention and risk factors: There is no known way to prevent or cure glaucoma but the disease is highly treatable and subject to control if caught early. Regular measurement of pressure in the eye by a physician is the key to success. Testing every two to five years is suggested for most people. People at specific risk for the disease, including African Americans, persons with diabetes mellitus, and those with a family history of chronic glaucoma, should be tested annually.

Glomerulonephritis

See **Kidney diseases**

Goiter

(GOY-tuhr)

DISEASE

TYPE: HORMONAL

See also
Asthma
Cancers
Diet and health
Endocrine system
Hormonal system
Hormone disorders
Thyroid gland

On the Internet
MEDLINE PLUS
www.nlm.nih.gov/medlineplus/ency/article/001178.htm

At the base of the neck, attached to the trachea (windpipe), is the thyroid. This endocrine gland produces the hormone thyroxin (thiy-ROK-sihn), essential for growth and metabolism. A goiter is an enlargement of the thyroid gland.

Cause: There are two types of goiter: simple and exophthalmic (EHK-suhf-THAAL-mihk). In simple goiter insufficient thyroxin is produced. This is usually due to insufficient iodine in the diet. Simple goiter can also be caused by certain medications, such as lithium, that prevent the synthesis of thyroid hormone. Apparently, thyroid tissue proliferates to enable more effective capture of whatever iodine is available.

In exophthalmic goiter there is an excessive production of thyroxin—a condition known as hyperthyroidism. Graves' disease is a type of hyperthyroidism. In this disorder antibodies mimicking the thyroid-stimulating hormone produced by the pituitary gland attack the thyroid, causing it to produce too much thyroxin.

Sometimes goiter is a symptom of another disease, such as the autoimmune disease *Hashimoto's thyroiditis* (THIY-roy-DIY-tihs), and it may disguise tumors of thyroid cancer.

Noticeable symptoms: Enlargement of the thyroid characterizes goiter. If goiter results from hyperthyroidism, additional symptoms will include rapid heart rate, nervousness, excessive sweating, increased appetite, weight loss, heat intolerance, fatigue, insomnia, and exophthalmos (bulging eyes). In some cases there will be difficulty in swallowing or breathing, symptoms that mimic other diseases such as throat cancer or asthma, which will need to be ruled out by tests of thyroid function.

Diagnosis: A doctor will perform a physical examination and tests to determine the amount of thyroxin being produced. Ultrasound will be used to determine if the thyroid tissue contains lumps or cysts. If there is any sign of lumps, further tests will be used to determine if they are benign, which is common, or cancerous, which is rare.

Treatment options: Most simple goiter can be treated by adding iodine to the diet. In some cases thyroxin is given to decrease the size of the thyroid.

Radioactive iodine, which destroys thyroid cells, may be administered for hyperthyroidism, or part of the thyroid may be removed surgically. An antithyroid medication to decrease thyroxin production may be prescribed.

Gonorrhea

(GON-uh-REE-uh)

DISEASE

TYPE: INFECTIOUS (BACTERIAL)

On the Internet
NATIONAL INSTITUTE OF ALLERGY AND INFECTIOUS DISEASES
www.niaid.nih.gov/factsheets/stdgon.htm

One of the most common bacterial diseases is sexually transmitted gonorrhea, sometimes called "clap" or "drip."

Cause: Gonorrhea is a highly infectious disease caused by a bacterium, *Neisseria gonorrhoeae,* and spread by sexual contact.

Incidence: Each year there are about 350,000 reported cases of gonorrhea in the United States, with at least another 370,000 cases estimated as unreported. The highest rates of infection in women are in 15 to 19 year olds; in men the highest rates are in 20 to 24 year olds.

Noticeable symptoms: Early symptoms in both men and women may be mild. In time, however, almost 90% of infected males show symptoms: frequent, painful urination and a thick whitish or yellowish discharge from the penis are the most common. About 80% of infected females experience no symp-

Gonorrhea may be limited to the genitals, but the bacteria can also enter the bloodstream, where they cause widespread damage. In men the most serious complication is heart disease; but women may also become sterile even without the bacteria spreading through the body; or the bacteria may cause blindness in a baby.

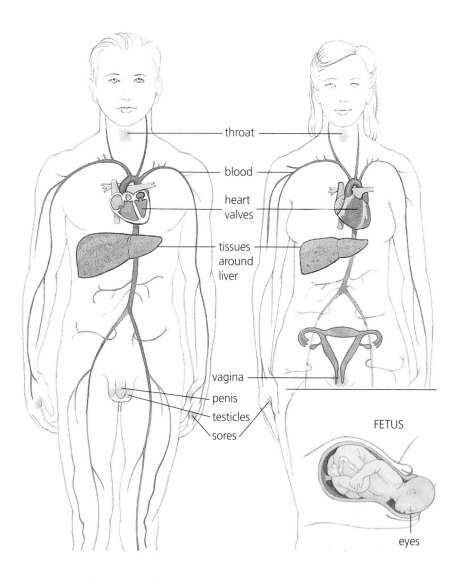

throat

blood

heart valves

tissues around liver

vagina

penis

testicles

sores

FETUS

eyes

toms. Those who have symptoms may have abdominal pain, frequent painful urination, vaginal bleeding after intercourse, and a thick discharge from the vagina. In both men and women the urethra may be irritated or swollen.

Diagnosis: Three tests for gonorrhea are currently in use: a urine test, microscopic examination of a smear of discharge, and a *culture* of samples from the urethra in males or cervix in females. Since none of these tests is completely accurate, physicians often conduct more than one test for a reliable diagnosis, usually beginning with the urine test.

Treatment options: Gonorrhea is treated with antibiotics taken in pill form or as an injection. It can now be treated with a single dose of medication taken when diagnosed. Penicillin was once the drug of choice to treat gonorrhea, but resistant forms of gonorrhea have developed. Today other, newer antibiotics are used to treat gonorrhea.

Stages and progress: Gonorrhea bacteria live and multiply in the mucous membranes of the body, especially of the penis, vagina, rectum, and throat. If the infection is untreated, bacteria spread to other areas of the body, including other parts of the reproductive system, causing complications. In men the result can be painful swelling of the penis and testicles, and in extreme cases sterility. In women the infection can lead to PID (pelvic inflammatory disease), a very painful condition that can damage the reproductive system. PID increases the risk of tubal pregnancies or sterility.

Gonorrhea bacteria can get into the bloodstream and spread throughout the body. The bacteria can cause arthritis and damage to the heart valves. Tissue around the liver can swell, causing pain in the abdomen. Sores can develop on the hands and feet. Because gonorrhea may be undetected in women at first, these rare complications are more common in females than in males.

If a pregnant woman has gonorrhea, it can affect her baby. During delivery the bacteria can infect the newborn, causing eye infections that, if untreated, can lead to blindness. In most states silver nitrate or other medication is placed in the eyes of newborns to guard against infection.

Prevention and risk factors: : The surest way to avoid gonorrhea is to abstain from sex. If this is not acceptable or not feasible, these tips help reduce risk:

- Stay in a relationship with only one person; be sure both of you have tested negative for sexually transmitted diseases;
- If not in a monogamous relationship, reduce the number of sex partners;
- Use a condom, correctly, with every partner, every time for every type of genital contact.

If you think you may have gonorrhea, prevent its spread to others by abstaining from sex until treatment results in a cure. If you are infected, encourage your sex partners to seek medical care. Also, do not rub your eyes after touching the infected area, as the bacteria can infect the eyes.

Gout

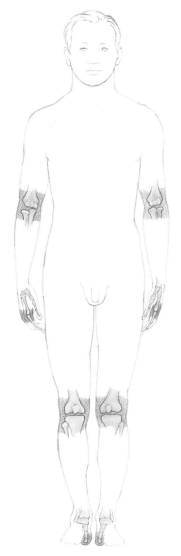

Although gout is famous for affecting the big toe, crystals of uric acid may lodge in any of the movable joints, causing inflammation and pain.

Gout, also called gouty arthritis, is one of the world's oldest known diseases. It is a type of arthritis and—like other types—is characterized by inflammation of one or more joints, which results in pain, swelling, and limited movement.

Cause: The swollen, painful joints that characterize gout result from a buildup of uric acid crystals in the cartilage separating the bones of a joint. Uric acid is produced during metabolism, when the body breaks down proteins. Although uric acid is insoluble, it is usually present in the form of very tiny particles that can be suspended in blood. Normally, these tiny particles are filtered out by the kidneys and suspended in urine, with which they leave the body harmlessly during urination.

People who suffer gout either produce more uric acid than average or, more commonly, fail to remove enough uric acid through their kidneys. The excess uric acid may combine with sodium to form crystals that inflame the patient's joints. The joint of the big toe is especially vulnerable. It is thought that the lower temperature of the toe, at the extremity of the body, facilitates formation of the crystals.

Incidence: Gout affects approximately 2.1 million people in the United States and up to 500,000 Canadians. It is much more common in men than women. It often affects men in their forties and fifties and among women is more common after menopause.

Noticeable symptoms: Sudden swelling and severe pain in joints of the feet, especially the joint at the base of the big toe, are telltale signs of gout. But attacks may also occur in elbows, knees, or joints of the hands. There are often red bumps, called *tophi* (TOH-fih), near the joints, bumps that hurt when they are pressed. Gout may also cause a fever as high as 101°F.

The first attack of gout usually disappears in a few days, even without treatment. But seeing a doctor is important because there are steps to take to prevent subsequent attacks.

Diagnosis: In making a diagnosis, gout needs to be distinguished from other forms of severe arthritis, such as rheumatoid arthritis. A family history of gout will make a physician suspicious, but testing for the characteristic high levels of uric acid in the blood is needed to confirm the diagnosis.

See also
Arthritis
Kidney and bladder stones
Kidney diseases
Kidneys

Drink water

Avoid alcohol

Treatment options: Though the pain and swelling that come with gout usually disappear after a time, the disorder should not be left untreated. With a doctor's care and a change in diet gout can usually be effectively controlled and new attacks prevented.

Reducing joint inflammation and pain are an important part of treating gout. For centuries doctors have used a drug called colchicine (KOHL-chih-SEEN), but today physicians prefer nonsteroidal anti-inflammatory and corticosteroid drugs because of fewer side effects.

Over the long term gout sufferers usually must take steps to control levels of uric acid in the body. For example, doctors may recommend drinking more water, cutting out alcohol, and avoiding certain protein-rich foods.

If attacks of gout continue, the physician may prescribe a drug to increase excretion of uric acid. Where high levels are already being excreted, doctors may instead decide to administer a drug that lowers uric acid production.

Stages and progress: Untreated gout eventually deforms the joints themselves and subjects the patient to long bouts of severe pain. Excessively high uric acid levels over the long term also lead to high blood pressure. Deposits of uric acid crystals may accumulate in the kidneys, resulting in kidney failure and death.

An unlikely status symbol

Strange as it may seem, gout was considered a sign of success and social status in the centuries before 1900. That was largely because the disorder was common among Europe's upper classes.

Gout did have an indirect connection with affluence. Wealthy noblemen could and did indulge themselves in large quantities of meat, starches, sweet wines, and the like—all of which helped raise their uric acid levels until an attack of gout was almost certain in those with a hereditary tendency toward the disorder. Poor people simply could not afford to set such a sumptuous table and so suffered the unpleasant reward—painful, debilitating gout—far less often.

Many famous people in history suffered with gout. Emperor Charles V, once one of Europe's most powerful rulers, abdicated in 1556 in part because he was tormented by gout. His son Philip II later endured crippling attacks of gout that forced him to rule Spain and Portugal from his bed. Other leading figures were gouty as well—English statesman William Pitt the Elder (and his son William Pitt the Younger), the famous lexicographer Samuel Johnson, and Methodist churchman John Wesley. Benjamin Franklin is numbered among America's most notable gout sufferers.

Graves' disease   *See* **Hormone disorders**

Growth

On the Internet
KIDS HEALTH
kidshealth.org/parent/medical/
endocrine/growth_disorder.html

Growth in humans can be separated into three main phases. The first phase—from a single fertilized egg to a school-age child—is extremely rapid as body and mind are formed. This is followed by a longer period, as a person progresses from childhood to adulthood, when physical and mental systems grow more slowly. The final phase, adulthood and old age, might be termed "negative growth," as bones become thinner, muscles shrink and weaken, and even the brain is reduced somewhat in size.

Childhood: The end of infancy can be said to occur when a child can walk and talk, typically around 2 years of age, although with considerable variability. From this time through the beginning of puberty, growth is often measured in terms of height, which typically increases from a base of about 35 inches at age 2 at a rate of 2 to 2.5 inches per year. Around the age of 11 for girls and 13 for boys, a sharp spurt in growth marks the beginning of adolescence. Another change is the loss of "baby teeth" between the ages of 6 and 12 and their replacement by permanent teeth.

In recent years many children around the world, but especially in industrialized nations, have grown rapidly in weight as well as height. Childhood obesity is thought to contribute to the development of diabetes mellitus, type 2, and heart disease. A program of exercise and sensible food choices are the chief weapons against obesity in children as well as adults.

Although children are susceptible to many minor infectious diseases, most of the more serious infectious diseases can be prevented by vaccinations. Another health issue is eyesight; many vision difficulties can be remedied at an early age.

The height of children varies widely. Some are shorter than normal because their parents are short—they represent one end of the range. In others early growth is slow but after the adolescent growth spurt, height catches up to normal. Some disorders interfere with growth. Two examples are the body alterations of Down syndrome and a genetic condition called *achondroplasia* (ay-KON-droh-PLAY-zhuh). In achondroplasia, the arms and legs are abnormally short, the spine is malformed, and the facial bones are misproportioned. Lack of human growth hormone

Sisters compare their heights, the most common way to look at growth. But the older sister is also beginning to experience other changes that occur when girls enter the teen years.

(HGH) also causes short stature. Growth-hormone deficiencies can be remedied by repeated injections of synthetic HGH during childhood. Additional hormone will not, however, increase the height of a person who is short for reasons unrelated to HGH.

Although childhood is normally thought of as a happy time, some children suffer from depression, while others face ADHD (attention deficit/hyperactivity disorder). These are usually treated with a combination of therapy and drugs.

Adolescence: The period between childhood and adulthood, known as adolescence, begins with puberty: the onset of sexual maturation. For boys, this corresponds roughly to the start of the teenage years; for girls puberty may begin as early as 11.

The development of secondary sexual characteristics is the most obvious sign of puberty. In girls, these characteristics include the development of breasts and wider hips, a higher-pitched voice, body hair, and an increase in the fat-to-muscle ratio. In boys, facial and body hair begin growing, the voice becomes lower in pitch, and muscle strength increases. Both sexes also experience growth spurts about this time.

Girls also experience the onset of menstruation, or monthly periods, toward the end of the changes of puberty. A cycle begins in which an egg is released from an ovary. If the egg is not fertilized, it dissolves and is shed along with the lining of the uterus and a small amount of blood. At this time, many girls also experience painful cramps. This cycle is repeated regularly, typically every 28 days, until a woman is in her forties or older. During the first half of this cycle, a female who engages in sexual intercourse is especially susceptible to pregnancy.

Boys have new experiences also toward the end of puberty. Normally, their penis grows longer and thicker during puberty. About the age of 13 or 14, they discover that sexual stimulation produces discharge of a fluid, termed ejaculation. This may occur during the night without sexual stimulation as well. The fluid is semen (SEE-muhn). By the end of puberty the semen contains active sperm.

Adolescence for many is a time of generally good health. A common experience is that adult teeth must be straightened with mechanical braces. Mental disorders can include depression and eating disorders. Other problems common in adolescents include acne, mononucleosis, and scoliosis.

Guillain-Barré syndrome

(gee-YAAN buh-RAY)

DISEASE

TYPE: AUTOIMMUNE

See also
Autoimmune diseases
Dysentery
Gastroenteritis
Influenza
Lyme disease
Mononucleosis
Paralysis
Vaccination and disease

On the Internet
NATIONAL INSTITUTE OF
NEUROLOGICAL DISORDERS AND
STROKE
www.ninds.nih.gov/disorders/
gbs/gbs.htm

Guillain-Barré syndrome, also called *acute inflammatory poly-neuropathy* (POL-ee-noo-ROP-uh-thee), is a rare form of muscle weakness or paralysis. It sometimes follows a viral or bacterial infection that is accompanied by a high fever (a *febrile* disease), such as viral gastroenteritis, influenza, or Lyme disease. Sometimes the condition is induced by vaccination or surgery.

Cause: The exact cause is unknown but the immune system sometimes reacts to a febrile infection (an infection accompanied by fever) with antibodies that attack the nervous system as well as the intended target. This attack damages the protective coating on nerves and causes weakness, numbness, and paralysis. The coating gradually grows back, restoring nerve operations.

Incidence: The disease is rare, affecting fewer than 3,000 persons each year in the United States. It can strike at any age but is most common in persons from 30 to 50 years old.

Symptoms: Fingers may feel strange and begin to curl up on their own. Similarly, legs and feet may feel tingly and then fail to work properly. As the weakness spreads, it may interfere with breathing and be accompanied by a faint feeling, rapid heartbeat, or sweating. These symptoms get progressiveworse rapidly over the course of a few days.

A physician will test for loss of nerve activity and look for evidence of a recent infection of one of the types associated with the disease or vaccination against influenza. The spinal fluid will show unusually high protein levels from the breakdown of the nerve covering.

Treatment options: Rest and physical therapy can help relieve symptoms. Injections of gamma globulin, a part of blood plasma containing antibodies, may slow down the progress of the disease. In severe attacks all the blood is removed (a little at a time) and cleansed of plasma and antibodies. If breathing is affected, a respirator may be used until the patient begins to recover.

Stages and progress: Muscles steadily weaken for two to four weeks. Thereafter nerves begin to rebuild their outer coats, taking months or years before all symptoms are gone. Fewer than 5% of cases lead to death.

Hair

REFERENCE

See also
Alcoholism
Anemia
Anorexia nervosa
Diet and health
Growth
Lice
Skin

On the Internet
P&G BEAUTY SCIENCE
www.pg.com/science/haircare/
hair_twh_toc.htm

Did You Know?
It is a myth that baldness is caused by wearing hats or caps. It's also a myth that shampoos or conditioners can cause baldness.

The average adult has about 5 million hairs. They cover almost every part of the body. Some, such as scalp hair, are easy to see, while others are so thin and small as to be almost invisible.

Each hair grows from a depression in the skin called a follicle. A hair consists of hundreds of flat, closely packed cells that gradually die as they move farther from their source of nourishment at the base of the follicle. Straight hair is round in cross-section and comes out of round follicles; curly hair is oval and is produced in oval follicles. Hair color is determined by the amount of a brownish-black pigment called melanin—the same pigment found in the outer layer of the skin. The greater the amount of melanin, the darker the hair. Factors such as hair color, hair width, forehead hairline, baldness, and hair type—straight and dense, tightly curled, silky, or wiry—are determined genetically.

Hair growth and head and body hair patterns change at different times of life. All the hair on an unborn baby's or young infant's scalp grows in at more-or-less the same time. A spurt of new hair growth occurs at the beginning of adolescence: Girls grow pubic, armpit, and leg hair; boys develop pubic, armpit, and facial hair.

After infancy, hair growth is not in unison: Shedding and growth occur concurrently among the many follicles in an area; that is, each hair has a life cycle of its own. Most hairs have a life of two to three years, though some last as long as six years. When a hair falls out, the follicle creates a new hair. But as a person ages, the follicles lose their ability to produce new hairs.

Hair and scalp conditions: On average, a person loses between 50 and 80 hairs a day. The amount of loss naturally increases as a person ages, resulting in baldness. Although baldness affects both men and women, it is more obvious in men; by the age of 50, about 50% of all men have lost some of their hair. In most cases, little can be done to avoid the thinning process. The compound Rogaine stops hair loss in some people and may even improve hair growth. People may choose to undergo hair transplants or hide thinning hair with wigs.

Taking care of hair properly involves keeping it clean. How frequently a person needs to shampoo and condition the hair depends on how dry or oily the hair is, and whether it is curly or straight.

In another type of hair loss, called diffuse hair loss, hair is lost from all parts of the body. The drugs used to treat cancer often cause diffuse hair loss, but the hair grows back after treatment stops. In other cases, diffuse hair loss may result from a thyroid disorder or other ailment. Individuals experiencing this problem should consult a doctor who can identify the cause.

Two common scalp conditions are dandruff, in which scales of dry or greasy skin flake off the skin, and infestations of tiny blood-sucking insects called head lice. Both problems can usually be resolved by using special shampoos.

Maintaining hair quality: Good health and a well-balanced diet help ensure healthy hair. Problems such as anemia, alcoholism, and starvation diets, such as those followed by people with anorexia nervosa, can cause poor hair growth and even hair loss.

Vitamin B_5, or panthenol, stimulates hair growth and improves its strength and glossiness. Hormones such as thyroid hormone and the sex hormones called androgens also stimulate growth. Steroids taken orally slow hair growth.

Ultraviolet radiation in sunlight as well as chemicals used to bleach or perm hair can damage hair's elasticity; as a result, hair will not hold its shape and will break easily. Hair's outer cuticle prevents water from entering or leaving the inner cortex. Excessive perming or tinting, or too much blow-drying, can damage the cuticle, drying out the hair and increasing the likelihood of split ends.

Hallucinations	*See* **Delusions**
Hangnails	*See* **Nail infections and injuries**
Hansen's disease	*See* **Leprosy**

Hantavirus diseases

DISEASE

TYPE: INFECTIOUS (VIRAL)

A new form of hemorrhagic fever—a fever accompanied by bleeding—was recognized in Asia in the 1950s. The virus that causes "Hantaan River disease" was finally identified in 1976 and named a hantavirus, for the Hantaan River in South Korea. In 1993 a series of deaths in the western United States led to recognition of another hantavirus disease, which came to be known as *hantavirus pulmonary syndrome* (HPS).

On the Internet
CENTERS FOR DISEASE CONTROL
AND PREVENTION (CDC)
www.cdc.gov/ncidod/diseases/
hanta/hps/

Hantavirus pulmonary syndrome begins when a person inhales dust that includes droppings from mice or other animals infected with hantavirus. When cleaning up a garage, outbuilding, or basement that might have been used by rodents, try to avoid stirring up dust.

Cause: Hantavirus diseases are caused by at least some members of the genus *Hantavirus*. Most often, these viruses are carried by rodents, although other animals—including lizards—have been found to harbor the viruses. Humans usually become infected by inhaling virus-contaminated aerosols of rodent excrement.

Incidence: HPS is a rare but serious and often fatal illness. Fewer than 40 cases are diagnosed annually in the United States. The disease has been confirmed in a majority of the U.S. states as well as in Canada and nations in Central and South America. Outbreaks correlate to both seasonal and year-to-year changes in rodent populations: Increased rodent population densities increase the number of human infections.

Noticeable symptoms: A hantavirus infection begins with fever and a cough, so that the early symptoms resemble influenza. As the disease progresses, the lungs suddenly fill with fluid, reducing the ability to breathe. The other serious symptom is bleeding, so hantavirus diseases are generally grouped among the diseases called hemorrhagic fevers.

Diagnosis: High white blood cell counts and low platelet counts indicate a serious infection, but more specific tests of antibodies in the blood must be used to establish that the infection is hantavirus disease.

Treatment options: Since this is a viral disease, treatment options are few. If a patient can be kept from suffocating from fluid filling the lungs or from kidney failure, natural antiviral reactions of the immune system eventually conquer the disease. Dialysis can be used to help a patient through kidney failure.

Stages and progress: After exposure to the virus in rodent droppings it may take from one to five weeks before flulike symptoms appear. HPS kills when blood plasma, not whole blood, leaks into the lungs. This may occur as early as one day after the coughing phase begins. After death the plasma-filled lungs can weigh twice as much as normal.

In Korean hemorrhagic fever blood leaks from the blood vessels while a high fever rages; death is caused by kidney failure.

Prevention and risk factors: Since HPS is transmitted only by droppings or saliva from rodents, especially the deer mouse, it is important to *avoid exposure to any rodent droppings.* If found, such droppings should be sprayed with a disinfectant and removed carefully. Ordinary household disinfectants dissolve the outer coat of the virus and thereby inactivate it. Rubber gloves can help in avoiding physical contact with the droppings.

Some instances of HPS appear to have started as a result of stirring up dust in places frequented by rodents. Avoid producing or breathing dust in places such as unused storage areas, little-used living spaces, and unoccupied cabins or lean-tos.

If a fever or cough should develop after exposure to dust from a place frequented by rodents, it is important to be examined by a physician. Tell your doctor that you may have been exposed to rodent dung or saliva.

Phone doctor

Hardening of the arteries

DISEASE

TYPE: MECHANICAL

See also
Aneurysm
Arteries
Atherosclerosis
Circulatory system
Dementia
Diabetes mellitus, type 2
Erectile dysfunction
Gangrene
Heart attack
Heart failure
Hypertension
Kidneys
Leg cramps
Stroke
TIA (transient ischemic attack)

As people grow older, the walls of their arteries usually become harder, stiffer, and less elastic. This is called hardening of the arteries, or *arteriosclerosis* (ahr-TEER-ee-oh-skluh-ROH-sihs). Often this occurs in one part of the body only, producing leg cramps in many cases and sometimes interfering with mental processes if the arteries are those that supply blood to the brain.

Cause: Healthy arteries are soft and elastic. With every beat of the heart they expand to receive blood and contract to help push blood through the body As people age, their arteries may become stiffer, less flexible, and less able to expand and contract. When this happens, the amount of blood that can pass through an artery decreases and, as a consequence, blood pressure increases.

Major factors in hardening of the arteries are atherosclerosis, cross-links between molecules, and calcium. In atherosclerosis the arteries become less flexible because their walls are thickened with deposits of fats and cholesterol, a combination called *plaque.* As time goes by, proteins and sugars in the artery walls form cross-links, a process similar to vulcanization of rubber. Calcium deposits form on artery walls.

Incidence: Most people over the age of 50 have some level of arteriosclerosis. The older a person is, the more likely that the disease exists—one out of five people over 64 have arteriosclerosis of the legs. Smokers are particularly at risk. Men are somewhat more likely than women to have hardening of the arteries, and the disease also seems to run in families.

Noticeable symptoms: If blood flow to the legs or feet is slowed or blocked, there may be aches and pains or heaviness and fatigue in the leg muscles or toes. This often occurs when exercising, climbing stairs, walking swiftly, or doing some other activity that puts a strain on the leg muscles. In some cases pain occurs even during rest.

Phone doctor

Since the heart has to work harder to push blood through the stiffened arteries, chest pains may occur. *See your physician if you experience either chest pains or pains in the legs or toes.* Short episodes of confusion or distortions in speech patterns may be the result of TIA (transient ischemic attacks), small strokes produced by arteriosclerosis of the arteries of the brain.

Treatment options: To help slow down the process of hardening of the arteries and its effects, stop smoking if you smoke, exercise, and stick to a low-fat, low-cholesterol diet.

Walking at a brisk pace is good for the heart and improves blood circulation in the legs. Walking causes some of the smaller arterial vessels to develop into alternate paths for the blood to take. These blood vessels then take over some of the work usually done by the larger arteries. This relieves the stress and strain on the stiff and narrowed larger arteries. A common treatment is to walk briskly until the legs hurt, rest until the pain recedes, and then walk briskly back to the starting point.

Your physician may also prescribe one or more types of medication. These may include vasodilating (VAA-zoh-diy-LAY-ting) drugs such as cilostazol (Pletal) to widen the arteries or anticlotting drugs, such as low doses of aspirin.

Exercise

Don't smoke

Prevention: Adopting healthy lifestyle practices while you are young may help prevent or delay hardening of the arteries. Refrain from smoking, eat a diet low in fats and cholesterol, and get plenty of aerobic exercise. Walking, running, jogging, swimming, tennis, and volleyball are good aerobic activities.

Harelip	*See* **Cleft lip and palate**
Hashimoto's disease	*See* **Hormone disorders**

Hay fever

DISEASE

TYPE: ALLERGY

See also
Allergies
Asthma
Autoimmune diseases
Immune system

On the Internet
MAYO CLINIC
www.mayoclinic.com/health/
hay-fever/DS00174

Every spring millions of people of all ages start sneezing almost on cue. These people do not have colds or the flu. They are just experiencing their annual bout of hay fever.

Cause: Hay fever, also called *allergic rhinitis* (riy-NIY-tihs), is an allergy to pollen or other airborne substances. Plants produce pollen in the spring. The pollen grains of some plants are so light that they float in the air and are inhaled by humans, causing hay fever in those who are sensitive. The most common irritants are pollens of such roadside plants as ragweed, sagebrush, and redroot pigweed. Many people are also allergic to grasses such as timothy, redtops, and rye. Various common trees also produce airborne pollens, including elms, maples, oaks, and birches. Other causes of hay fever include floating bits of mold, dust, and dandruff from animals.

Any substance that provokes an allergic reaction is an *allergen* (AAL-uhr-juhn). Breathing air containing an allergen causes a reaction in people who respond to that substance. The body treats the allergen as if it were an invader and produces substances to fight it. In hay fever the immune system fights with a compound called *histamine,* which causes most hay fever symptoms.

Incidence: Over 30 million people in North America react to pollen or other airborne allergens by developing hay fever symptoms, usually during spring or summer.

Noticeable symptoms: The most common symptom is sneezing, often combined with a stuffy head, runny nose, or watery or itchy eyes. Headache or an itchy feeling on the inside of the nose, mouth, and throat may also be signs of hay fever.

Diagnosis: The first step is to determine exactly when symptoms occur. Different pollens are in the air at different times; for example, in the United States oak trees usually release pollen in February and March in the South and in April and May in the North.

When engaged in indoor occupations, air conditioning can help prevent the pollen from such plants as ragweed, sagebrush, or redroot pigweed from provoking hay fever.

Phone doctor

A physician called an *allergist* may use a skin test to find out exactly which allergen is involved. The allergist injects small amounts of each suspected allergen under the skin and watches for a reaction. If the allergen causes a small bump with a red ring around it, it is likely an allergic reaction. However, skin tests are not always accurate. A newer test is based on a blood sample from the patient and measures how much histamine the blood releases in response to the suspected allergen.

Some medicines may produce hay fever symptoms as a side effect. A physician will consider this possibility as well.

Prevention and complications: The best way to prevent symptoms of hay fever is by avoiding the allergen. Some even travel to a different region during hay fever season. But there are ways to reduce risk at home, such as keeping house and car windows closed and using an air conditioner; staying inside during the morning when most pollen is in the air; and, if possible, finding someone to mow the lawn and rake leaves. A filtration mask and safety goggles can protect against the allergen when it is necessary to work outside. Do not put sheets and towels outside to dry; use a clothes dryer so that pollen cannot collect on the cloth.

If hay fever begins to be accompanied by difficulty in breathing and a tight feeling in the chest, see a physician. About 5 to 10% of all persons with hay fever also develop asthma, a more serious disease that begins as difficulty in breathing. If hay fever persists for several years, a physician should examine the nose for polyps, which can become harmful if not treated.

Treatment options: Antihistamines (AAN-tee-hihs-tuh-MEENZ) reduce hay fever symptoms by blocking the action of histamine. Over-the-counter antihistamines have side effects, including drowsiness, so use them with care. Prescription antihistamines produce less drowsiness. Decongestants, which relieve most sinus and nasal congestion, can also be taken but many of them are not recommended for people with hypertension. Nasal sprays containing steroids or chemicals such as cromolyn sodium also can be effective in controlling hay fever.

When hay fever is severe, allergy injections may be required. The allergist will inject a series of shots. Each injection contains a small amount of the allergens that are causing hay fever. Exposure to these small doses can produce tolerance to the allergen. The body will stop reacting to the allergen as if it were an invader, and hay fever symptoms cease. The full course of allergy injections must be continued for several years to be completely effective.

Headache

On the Internet
NATIONAL INSTITUTE OF NEUROLOGICAL DISORDERS AND STROKE
www.ninds.nih.gov/disorders/headache/headache.htm

Headache—pain felt in the region surrounding the brain—is a common symptom. Almost everyone has headaches at least occasionally and many people have them once a month or more. Headache is not within the brain itself. Rather, it originates in the covering of the brain or in other tissues surrounding the brain, most often the muscles of the upper head.

While diseases or injuries cause some headaches, other headaches are disorders in their own right. For example, *tension headaches* are believed to result from prolonged contraction of muscles in the head, neck, or upper back. *Vascular headaches* are caused by a sudden widening (dilation) of arteries serving the head. The best-known form of vascular headache is migraine, but others include cluster headaches and temporal arteritis. Some headaches caused by infections also involve dilation of arteries in the head.

Cause: Conditions that cause headache include alcohol poisoning (hangover); brain tumor; carbon monoxide poisoning; bacterial or viral infections such as encephalitis, influenza, Lyme disease, meningitis, mononucleosis, and the common cold; head injury; kidney failure; and stroke. The muscle contractions that cause tension headaches may result from faulty posture or habits such as clenching the jaws or tensing the back or neck.

Noticeable symptoms: Headache may affect the whole top of the head or only particular areas. Tension headaches are typically dull, steady aches, often occurring on both sides of a specific area such as the forehead. Migraine is a throbbing or stabbing pain that tends to affect only one side of the head. Headaches caused by colds tend to concentrate around the eyes and forehead.

Headaches may be accompanied by additional symptoms depending on the cause. For example, migraine is often accompanied by nausea, and a cluster headache causes running of the eye and nose on the affected side.

Relief of symptoms: Tension headaches are commonly treated with painkillers of two main kinds: nonsteroidal anti-inflammatory drugs (NSAIDs) such as aspirin, ibuprofen, or naproxen; or the pain relief drug acetaminophen. Stronger, prescription NSAIDs, such as COX-2 inhibitors, are used only in cases of severe, frequently recurrent, and long-lasting headaches. The drug ergotamine (also known as ergot) counters the dilation of the blood vessels but must be taken in exactly the right dose and absorbed into the system at the very beginning of an attack. A pregnant woman should not take ergotamine since it raises the risk of miscarriage, but the milder drug isometheptine (Midrin) may be a satisfactory substitute.

Phone doctor

Physical methods, such as warm compresses or ice packs, massage, and rest, may also be effective. Tension headaches often subside after a good night's rest.

Prevention and possible actions: Most headaches are acute, temporary conditions. They either go away by themselves or quickly respond to painkilling medications. *If you suffer a headache that is unusually severe or long lasting, or is accompanied by unusual sensations (such as numbness) in other parts of your body, consult a doctor.* The headache may be a symptom of some other disease or injury that requires prompt medical attention. Stroke, for example, may begin as a severe headache that starts suddenly.

Practice meditation

Tension headaches can sometimes be prevented by posture correction or other physical therapy. But the best approach may be to reduce the physical response to psychological stress through stress-management techniques such as relaxation exercises, meditation, and biofeedback.

Head injuries

INJURY

Phone doctor

Any hard blow to the head can cause potentially dangerous injury to the brain. Therefore the rule to follow is one of caution: *See your doctor after any hard blow to the head, especially if you have been knocked unconscious or show any signs of mental impairment afterward.*

Cause: Brain tissue itself may be damaged by a hard blow, especially one that fractures (breaks) the skull. Another danger

BRAIN DAMAGE

Brain damage days after a head injury can come from a slow leak that produces either an epidural or a subdural hematoma. Symptoms can include headache, unequal pupil sizes, and nausea. Get medical help immediately when such symptoms occur after an accident.

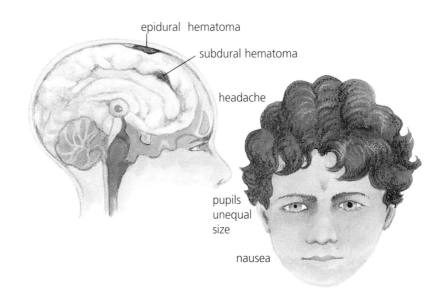

epidural hematoma

subdural hematoma

headache

pupils unequal size

nausea

Emergency Room

from fracture is infection of brain tissue. Even if the skull is not fractured, a broken artery between the outer covering of the brain and the skull can produce considerable bleeding in a small, closed-in region. Without medical treatment to relieve the bleeding, pressure on the brain can build to such a level that permanent brain damage or death can occur. Other types of serious brain damage stem from swelling of the brain and leakage of cerebrospinal (SEHR-uh-broh-SPIY-nuhl) fluid.

Incidence: Each year millions of people sustain head injuries. In the United States more than 500,000 of these injuries require hospitalization. Leading causes of head injuries include traffic accidents, falls, physical assaults, and accidents at home, work, outdoors, or while playing sports.

Noticeable symptoms: Loss of consciousness, even briefly, may indicate that a blow was hard enough to cause potentially serious brain damage. Other warning signs include persistent headache; disturbed sleep; persistent drowsiness, confusion, or stupor; vomiting; difficulty in speaking or breathing; memory loss; difference in the size of the eyes' pupils; seizures or partial paralysis; prolonged unconsciousness or coma; bruising around the eyes or behind the ears; and blood or clear fluids leaking from the ears or nose. *A person experiencing these symptoms after being hit in the head—whether immediately or hours or days after the blow—should see a doctor as soon as possible.*

Diagnosis: Diagnosis can be difficult because outward symptoms often do not appear immediately. The doctor will examine the person's eyes and check alertness and ability to concentrate. The doctor may order skull x-rays or a CT scan to check for skull fracture and brain injury, including leaking or clotted blood.

A hematoma (HEE-muh-TOH-muh) is an accumulation of blood that has leaked out of damaged blood vessels. In a subdural (suhb-DOOR-uhl) hematoma, bleeding occurs between the brain's outer layer and the tissue beneath it. An epidural (EHP-ih-DOOR-uhl) hematoma traps blood between the skull and the brain.

Call ambulance

Treatment options: Emergency first aid may be vital for severe head injuries. ***Call for emergency assistance immediately.*** The injured person should lie down and remain quiet until help arrives. Cover any head wound but do not apply pressure or attempt to clean it. ***Do not move the patient if you suspect a broken neck or back.*** Otherwise use a pillow or blanket to elevate the person's shoulders and head slightly. Do not give any medication without a doctor's approval.

Any head injury requires monitoring. If a person with a head injury wants to sleep soon after, wake him or her every two to three hours and check for mental confusion. Most cases of slight head injury heal by themselves after two to three days. But if a person has been knocked unconscious for two minutes or more, a hospital stay for a day or two is often required even if there are no immediate signs of injury. During this period the hospital staff can monitor any change in condition.

Treatment depends on the nature of the injury. Doctors may use intravenous medications, surgery, or a combination of the two. If there is bleeding inside the head, doctors use medication to try to keep pressure from building on the brain. Surgery may be required to relieve pressure, remove a hematoma, realign broken bone, or remove a bullet or other foreign object that has penetrated the skull.

Prevention: Routine safety precautions can prevent many common causes of head injury. For example, always wear a seat belt when traveling in a car. Wear a helmet when riding a bicycle or a motorcycle, skateboarding, or during other recreational activities involving possible head injury. Occupations with a high risk of head injury call for protective headgear. When balance appears to be shaky, as in many older persons, rails in bathrooms and other locations can help prevent falls.

Heart

The heart, the central pump of the circulatory system, consists of four muscular pockets called *chambers.* Blood from the body enters the chamber known as the *right atrium* (AY-tree-uhm). The blood is then pumped through a valve to a larger chamber below the atrium called the *right ventricle.* The right ventricle forces the blood into an artery leading to the lungs. After taking in oxygen in the lungs and leaving carbon dioxide behind, the blood returns to the heart, entering the *left atrium.* There blood is squeezed through a valve into the *left ventricle,* the heart's largest chamber and most powerful pump. The left ventricle pushes the blood into the arteries that lead to the body.

Size and location: The heart's size is often compared to a person's fist—larger people tend to have both larger fists and larger hearts. A much enlarged heart is a sign of poor health. The heart enlarges when it has had to work too hard, usually as a result of diseases of the circulatory system compounded by obesity.

The heart is in the upper middle of the chest, just barely off center on the left side of the body. It sounds louder on the left because the powerful left ventricle makes most of the sound of a heartbeat. Often a heart attack is marked by pain that travels up the left arm.

Role: The heart is primarily a pump that pushes the blood through the blood vessels. If the heart stops beating or otherwise cannot fulfill its function, death follows rapidly.

The heart is also an endocrine gland, secreting a hormone that, along with other hormones from the kidneys and endocrine glands, helps regulate blood pressure.

Conditions that affect the heart: The most direct effect on the heart comes from blockages, such as atherosclerosis or embolism, that prevent oxygenated blood from reaching heart muscle, causing the muscle to die. The general name for sudden loss of heart action from such causes is heart attack. Heart attack and the slower developing and more persistent heart failure, which is often caused by atherosclerosis as well, are the leading causes of death in most industrialized countries.

Like other organs, the heart is subject to infection, especially by bacteria, which can interfere with the valves and other operations of the heart. For example, when "strep" bacteria cause the general infection known as *rheumatic fever* there is often perma-

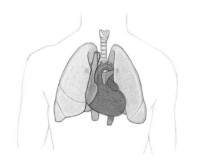

The heart is just slightly to the left of the midline of the body, nestled into the left lung, which is smaller than the right.

Use CPR

The heart combines two pumps, one that moves blood to the lungs and back with one that propels blood throughout the body.

nent heart damage. Persons who already have damaged valves, or heart murmur, are especially susceptible to bacterial infection of the heart and need to take special precautions to avoid it.

Some generalized chronic diseases affect the heart as well as other organs, notably diabetes mellitus. Hypertension is often the cause of heart disease as well as of other serious organ failures.

The heart is susceptible to various genetic and developmental problems as well. Some, such as *aortic stenosis,* a narrowing of the valve that controls flow of blood out of the heart into the body, are strictly diseases of the heart, while others, such as Down syndrome or Marfan syndrome, are pervasive disorders that usually affect the heart along with other organs.

A wound to the heart is among the most dangerous of events, usually resulting in death in a matter of moments. Electric shock can also stop a heart from beating.

In many cases a heart that has been stopped from beating for a brief period can be restarted. The technique is part of *cardiopulmonary resuscitation* (CPR), a method easily learned in special classes that are generally available. Emergency health workers also use electrical devices that can restore a heartbeat.

Prevention of heart disease: Although heart disease is the leading cause of death, the incidence of death from heart attack or heart failure in the United States has fallen more than 30% since 1990. The exact cause of the decline is not known to a certainty, but it is assumed that the population is increasing the practices known to reduce heart disease. These include stopping tobacco

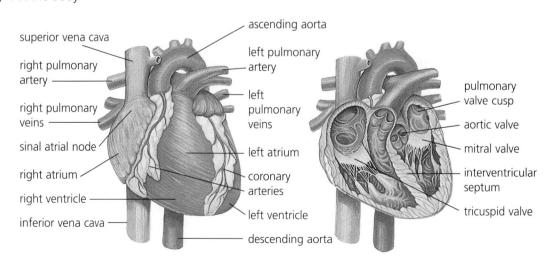

superior vena cava
right pulmonary artery
right pulmonary veins
sinal atrial node
right atrium
right ventricle
inferior vena cava
ascending aorta
left pulmonary artery
left pulmonary veins
left atrium
coronary arteries
left ventricle
descending aorta
pulmonary valve cusp
aortic valve
mitral valve
interventricular septum
tricuspid valve

use and lowering alcohol use to moderate levels; eating a low-fat and low-cholesterol diet; exercising regularly, including incorporating such activities as gardening or active sports such as tennis; and reducing hypertension with either diet or drugs.

Heart attack

DISEASE

TYPE: MECHANICAL

See also
Angina
Arrhythmias
Atherosclerosis
Heart
Heart failure
Mitral stenosis and incompetence
Pericarditis

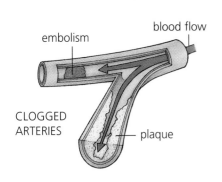

embolism
blood flow

CLOGGED
ARTERIES
plaque

A heart attack occurs when blood supply to an area of the heart is reduced or stopped and heart muscle tissue dies. The medical term for heart attack is *myocardial infarction* (MIY-oh-KAHR-dee-uhl ihn-FAHRK-shun). *Myocardium* is a term for heart muscle. An *infarct* is an area of dead tissue.

Cause: Heart attacks are the direct result of *coronary artery disease,* or atherosclerosis of the arteries of the heart. When fatty deposits called *plaque* narrow coronary (heart) arteries, blood flow is reduced, which can damage the heart. When blood flow to the heart is obstructed, the heart muscle tissue does not get enough oxygen. An acute attack occurs when a clot breaks loose and blocks the narrowed coronary artery, killing cells in the heart normally supplied with blood by that artery.

Incidence and risk factors: Heart attacks are the leading cause of death in the United States, where there are over 1.2 million each year. In nearly three out of four cases, however, the individual is still alive a year after the initial attack.

More than 50% of all heart attacks and 83% of deaths from heart disease occur in people over 65, although 30% of sudden deaths between the ages of 14 and 21 stem from heart attacks. Women under 65 have fewer heart attacks than men of the same age.

Risk factors for heart attack include smoking, obesity, a diet high in fats and cholesterol, lack of exercise, stress, high blood pressure, diabetes, or a family history of heart disease.

Noticeable symptoms: The most common sign of a heart attack is a severe crushing pain accompanied by feelings of tightness or squeezing in the chest or upper abdomen. This pain usually lasts about five to fifteen minutes or more. It may spread to the left arm, the shoulders, neck, or jaw. Often a person has cold sweats and a rapid or irregular pulse just before an attack. Other symptoms include anxiety, fatigue, nausea,

Call ambulance

On the Internet
AMERICAN ACADEMY
OF FAMILY PHYSICIANS
familydoctor.org/291.xml

vomiting, and shortness of breath. A heart attack is a life-threatening emergency. Most fatalities occur within the first two hours of the attack. *An ambulance should be called at the very first symptoms.* Taking a regular aspirin tablet during a heart attack can help prevent further clotting.

In about 20% of heart attacks there are no symptoms. These may be discovered later during a complete medical examination.

Diagnosis: A physician will use a stethoscope to detect any abnormal heart sounds and will check pulse rate and blood pressure. A series of *electrocardiograms* (ECGs) will be done to see if there are any irregularities in heartbeat. An ECG can also identify a blocked coronary artery. Blood samples will be taken over a few days. A high level of cardiac enzymes in the blood is an indicator of damaged heart muscle. Other diagnostic tests will be employed to pinpoint the location and the extent of damage to heart tissue.

Treatment options: Often emergency workers use special paddles to apply an electric current to an individual's chest to restore a regular heartbeat or to restart a stopped heart. One of the first drugs to be administered may be a clot buster, such as streptokinase. Given within one to two hours after the start of an attack, clot busters can significantly reduce heart attack fatalities. Aspirin or heparin is often given to prevent further clotting. Other drugs may be used to overcome any irregularity in the heart's rhythm, to strengthen heart muscle, or to expand the arteries and ease the heart's workload. Morphine is commonly injected for pain. Surgery may be necessary to clean out and reopen or replace diseased arteries.

Much more than a headache remedy

Aspirin was introduced over a century ago as an effective treatment for fever and a mild pain reliever. Today aspirin has become a key drug in the treatment of heart problems. Because it prevents platelets in the blood from forming clots, aspirin is commonly prescribed for people who have had a heart attack or stroke. Given within the first 24 hours of a heart attack, aspirin can reduce the number of deaths by 23%. Individuals at risk for heart disease may, on a physician's advice, take small doses of aspirin daily.

Aspirin is not for everyone, however. It can be dangerous when given to children and can cause stomach upset or even internal bleeding in adults.

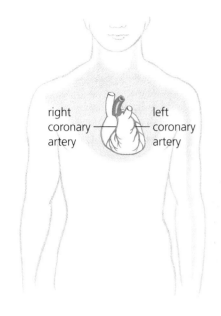

right coronary artery

left coronary artery

Pain from a heart attack often radiates beyond the center of the chest to reach the shoulders and neck. Sometimes it travels down the left arm, but it may also be felt in the right. If you have doubt about whether chest pain is a heart attack, you should assume that it is one and seek prompt medical assistance.

A person who is having a heart attack or who has just had one is usually confined to bed rest in the coronary care unit of a hospital. A heart attack victim may also be given oxygen for the first day or two. Once out of danger, the patient can be moved to a regular hospital room. Over a period of two to three weeks the patient will begin to resume some activities. The physician will probably prescribe a cardiac rehabilitation program. It may include restrictions on smoking, changes in diet, drug therapy, an exercise regimen, and other lifestyle changes.

Prevention: The best way to prevent a heart attack is to adopt lifestyle habits that help bar the development of atherosclerosis. A physician may prescribe a daily dose of "baby aspirin" or "regimen aspirin" (81 mg daily) to prevent blood clot problems.

Heartburn

SYMPTOM

Heartburn is a distinctive burning pain that feels as if it comes from behind the breastbone, where the heart is. But the pain has nothing to do with the heart at all. The true source is in the esophagus, at the point where it connects with the stomach. The pain is transferred, or referred, from this source to the chest.

Cause: The direct cause of the pain is irritation of the esophagus lining by acid and other digestive juices from the stomach. Ordinarily, a ring of muscle called the lower esophageal sphincter (LES) contracts to prevent the strongly acid contents of the stomach from backing up into the esophagus. But sometimes the sphincter muscle abnormally relaxes, allowing some of the contents to escape—an effect called gastroesophageal reflux. The esophagus, unlike the stomach, has no protective layer of mucus to keep it from becoming irritated, and the result is intense, intermittent pain.

Two natural conditions make heartburn especially prevalent among pregnant women. First, throughout pregnancy a higher than usual level of the female hormone progesterone tends to

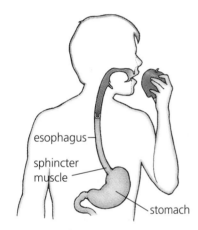

esophagus

sphincter muscle

stomach

The lining of the esophagus is not protected against stomach fluids. Pain in the chest occurs if fluids rise into the esophagus.

On the Internet

NATIONAL HEARTBURN ALLIANCE

www.heartburnalliance.org/

relax muscles of many kinds, including the sphincter muscle of the esophagus. Second, late in pregnancy the presence of the developing fetus in an enlarged uterus presses the stomach upward, increasing the likelihood that some of the contents will be forced upward into the esophagus.

Some cases of heartburn may be caused by another disorder, a hiatal hernia. The diaphragm that separates the chest from the abdomen has a small opening, or hiatus, through which the esophagus passes to the stomach. If the opening is abnormally large, part of the stomach may bulge through it, forming a hernia. As a result, the sphincter muscle of the esophagus may not be able to function properly.

Less common sources of heartburn are failure of the LES to open, thus causing food or fluids to collect in the esophagus; the autoimmune disease scleroderma, which may attack the lining of the esophagus; and diseases that cause overproduction of stomach acid.

Incidence: Heartburn is extremely common. About 60 million Americans and 8 million Canadians experience it, 25% of them daily. It is less common in nonindustrialized nations. The symptom affects about one in four of all pregnant women.

Noticeable symptoms: The attacks of burning chest pain are intermittent—they last a few minutes, with brief intervals of relief in between. During an attack, the victim may cough up a little sour-tasting stomach fluid into the back of the mouth. Since backflow into the esophagus is easier when one is lying down, attacks may tend to occur at night; getting up may make the sufferer feel better. If the pain ceases, then heartburn is almost surely the cause. Another sign of the disorder is relief soon after taking an antacid.

Those who have chronic heartburn may also experience hoarseness, coughing, wheezing, and swallowing difficulties from repeated inflammation of the esophagus.

Diagnosis: The two most common tests that physicians use to confirm the diagnosis and to assess the damage to the esophagus are the barium-swallow x-ray and endoscopy (ehn-DOS-kuh-pee). Barium is opaque to x-rays; when a solution of it is swallowed during x-ray examination, it reveals irregularities in the esophagus caused by acid erosion. An endoscope is a microscope on the end of a narrow, flexible fiberoptic tube. The instrument is lowered through the throat to the bottom of the esophagus to look for inflammation and damage.

Treatment options: First aid for a heartburn attack is an antacid to neutralize the acid in the esophagus. It works almost immediately, but its effects last only a couple of hours. It is often combined with an H_2 blocker drug such as cimetidine (Tagamet), famotidine (Pepcid), or ranitidine (Zantac); these reduce the production of stomach acid for several hours.

Those who suffer frequent, persistent attacks may be prescribed a drug called a proton pump inhibitor, such as omeprazole (Prilosec), usually taken once a day. These drugs do not relieve attacks but tend to prevent them.

Lifestyle changes, such as losing weight, can also help head off attacks or make them less severe. In addition a number of substances generate extra stomach acid or tend to relax the sphincter muscle. These include caffeine (particularly in coffee, but also in tea and cola drinks), alcohol, tobacco, greasy and spicy foods, onions and garlic, chocolate, mints (peppermint, spearmint, etc.), and NSAID painkillers such as aspirin and ibuprofen.

No caffeine   Avoid alcohol

Avoid aspirin

Attacks at night may be headed off by raising the head of the bed four to six inches from the floor, so that the esophagus is elevated above the stomach. Using extra pillows is not enough—at least the upper half of the body must be raised. Blocks under the upper end of the bed so that the whole bed tilts, or a foam wedge under the upper part of the mattress may do the trick. Avoiding lying down for at least two hours after eating, when the stomach is still emptying, is also advisable.

Heartburn during pregnancy is difficult to cope with because many pregnant women and their physicians prefer not to use medications unless absolutely necessary. One possible remedy is to eat frequent small meals each day rather than two or three large ones.

If not controlled, frequent acid irritation from chronic heartburn may do permanent damage to the esophagus. In a small minority, cells in the esophagus may mutate and become cancerous. Chronic heartburn is the most common symptom of gastroesophageal reflux disease, or GERD. Only in cases of severe, prolonged GERD is surgery used, to strengthen the sphincter or to remedy damage to the esophagus.

Heart failure

DISEASE

TYPE: MECHANICAL

On the Internet
AMERICAN HEART ASSOCIATION
www.americanheart.org/
presenter.jhtml?identifier=1486

Heart failure is the term used when the heart's pumping action becomes weak and inefficient. When heart muscle has been damaged by an underlying disorder, the heart's ability to contract and push out blood to the rest of the body is weakened. The heart also has difficulty filling up with blood between contractions. Blood accumulates in the veins leading to the heart or from the lungs. The veins become overloaded, and fluid seeps out into the lungs or into other body organs and tissues.

Cause: Hypertension (high blood pressure) is one of several conditions that weaken or damage heart muscle by making the heart pump harder, which causes the heart to enlarge and its muscle tissue to weaken. A narrowed valve also forces the heart to push harder. Lung diseases that impede circulation through the lungs have the same effect. Thyroid disorders may make the heart pump faster, which also enlarges the muscle.

The heart may be damaged in other ways. Alcohol abuse takes its toll on the heart as well as on the liver, and tobacco use injures the heart as well as the lungs. Sometimes the heart is damaged by *cardiomyopathies* (heart muscle diseases), which can be caused by infection, genetic disorders, or other conditions.

Incidence: Heart failure affects 5 million Americans. Each year about 550,000 new cases are diagnosed in the United States, and nearly 60,000 die from heart failure. It also contributes to 300,000 deaths from other diseases annually. Death rates are somewhat higher for African Americans than for whites.

Heart failure can occur in people of any age. It is more common, however, after age 50 and is the leading cause of hospitalization for those 65 or over. At age 40 the lifetime risk of developing heart failure reaches one in five.

Noticeable symptoms: The most common symptoms are a progressive shortening of the breath—first while exercising and later during the least of exertions—or swelling in the extremities caused by fluid buildup (edema) or both.

Sometimes heart failure affects one side of the heart more than the other, so we speak of *left-sided heart failure* or *right-sided heart failure*. When organs and tissues become congested with fluid, the condition is called *congestive heart failure*.

Phone doctor

- In left-sided heart failure fluid accumulates in the lungs. This causes shortness of breath and fatigue. At first this may happen only during physical activity; later it can happen when lying down. It may even be necessary to sleep sitting up. If the lungs become very congested, there may be bubbling sounds and pain in the chest. A persistent cough may bring up pinkish mucus. *Fluid accumulation in the lungs is a dangerous condition and requires prompt treatment by a physician.* Pneumonia is a common complication when fluid buildup has occurred.
- In right-sided heart failure there is usually edema, or swelling, of the feet, ankles, or legs. There may be pain in the lower part of the back or the abdomen due to swelling of the liver or other internal organs. Fluid buildup often results in sudden weight gain. The kidneys may have difficulty in handling the accumulation of fluid and salt, and kidney failure may occur.
- In congestive heart failure both sets of symptoms occur together. There may also be dementia and loss of appetite. Muscles may waste away, although weight and general body shape may remain constant.

When heart failure is severe, there may also be a very rapid or irregular heartbeat.

Treatment options: A low-salt diet and taking a diuretic to increase urination lowers fluid buildup, which reduces blood volume. Other medicines expand blood vessels. When blood flows more easily, the heart does not have to work as hard. Alcohol and tobacco use should be stopped or severely limited. If these steps do not produce enough relief, digitalis [DIHJ-ih-TAAL-ihs] (digoxin) may be prescribed to slow the heart rate and to strengthen heart muscle contractions. Digitalis requires careful monitoring, as too much can be deadly. If narrowed valves or arteries are the cause of heart failure, surgery can often correct that underlying problem. A heart transplant may be the only recourse for advanced cases.

The overall outlook depends on the underlying cause and the severity of the problem. About 10% of heart failure patients die within the first year of the initial diagnosis. Over 40% die within four to five years. If treatment is early and successful, however, a person with heart failure can lead a long and normal life.

Don't smoke

Avoid alcohol

Heart murmur

SYMPTOM

See also
Atrial fibrillation
Congenital heart defects
Endocarditis
Heart
Heart failure
Inflammation
Prolapse of mitral valve

On the Internet
KIDS HEALTH
kidshealth.org/parent/medical/
heart/murmurs.html

A physician using a stethoscope to listen to the heart may hear sounds other than the normal "lub-dub" of the beating heart. These extra sounds are called heart murmurs. They are the sounds of the four heart valves opening and closing or of blood flowing turbulently through the heart.

The valves normally open and close in a synchronized way so blood is kept flowing in only one direction through the heart. When heart valves are working perfectly, they are almost silent. If the physician hears murmurs, which may sound like flutters, clicks, gallops, or knocks, something may be wrong with one or more valves. Often, however, the sounds are *innocent heart murmurs,* so called because they are produced by perfectly healthy hearts. Innocent murmurs occur frequently in children, thin people, athletes, and pregnant women.

Parts affected: When a heart murmur signifies a disorder or defect in one or more of the four heart valves, it may indicate a narrowing of the opening (*stenosis*), blood flowing the wrong way through one or more of the valves (*regurgitation),* or a failure in the way the valves close (*prolapse*). Inflammation of the heart muscle may also produce a heart murmur.

Related symptoms: When a structural defect or disease of the heart is the cause of a heart murmur, there may be additional symptoms. Depending on the problem, these may include vague chest pains, fatigue, shortness of breath, cough, irregular heartbeats, or fainting episodes.

Associations: Rheumatic fever, congenital heart defects, or the process of aging can cause stenosis, a narrowing and stiffening of heart valves. In stenosis valves do not open completely; hence blood does not flow forward freely and backs up. Aging and endocarditis, an inflammation of the valve lining, may cause "leady" (like the soft metal lead) valves. Valves fail to close properly and blood regurgitates, or leaks back, into one of the heart chambers. Mitral valve prolapse, a relatively common deformity of the heart's mitral valve, may occasionally produce some leakage. The added difficulty of making blood flow properly through the heart may lead to a form of irregular heartbeat called atrial fibrillation.

Bacteria that live in the mouth or intestines and cause no

damage there can travel in the bloodstream to the heart, where they often infect a damaged valve. This can lead to the serious heart disease endocarditis. If a person has a heart murmur, taking antibiotics before dental or intestinal surgery is recommended to prevent serious heart damage.

Relief of symptoms: Medicines called beta blockers slow heartbeat, enabling blood to be processed by valves that have only slight damage. If there is atrial fibrillation, steps need to be taken to prevent clots from forming. Heart valves may need surgical repair or replacement. A narrowed valve can sometimes be opened with a form of balloon angioplasty. Valve replacement, which may be with an artificial valve or with a pig's heart valve, also requires the patient with the new valve to take blood thinners to prevent clots.

Heat stroke and exhaustion

DISEASE

TYPE: MECHANICAL

See also
Fever
Sunburn

On the Internet
UNIVERSITY OF MARYLAND MEDICAL CENTER
www.umm.edu/non_trauma/dehyrat.htm

Every summer millions of Americans suffer heat-related disorders. These range from simple fatigue caused by prolonged heat to the most dangerous, heat stroke, sometimes known as *sunstroke*.

Cause: When the temperature of a person's blood rises above its normal range, the *hypothalamus*, a control center in the brain, sends a signal to the heart to pump more blood and to enlarge the blood vessels, particularly those in the skin. As more blood flows through the enlarged vessels, some excess heat passes into the cooler air. If this is not enough to cool the blood, sweat glands begin to pour out water, which evaporates from the skin, carrying more heat away. Sweating cools skin, but excess loss of fluids and salts (electrolytes) in sweat can change blood chemistry and lead to heat exhaustion.

If air temperature is as high as blood temperature, or if hot sunlight is pouring onto the skin, blood does not cool as it circulates through the skin. When the humidity rises to 60%, sweat does not evaporate. Body temperature begins to rise. When the body's cooling mechanism is overtaxed, the overheated brain can no longer function normally; this is the main danger of heat stroke.

Incidence: In an ordinary summer, about 400 Americans die from heat stroke—more than from all other weather-related conditions combined. Around the world, heat waves have resulted in much higher death totals, often in the thousands. Global warming is thought to be increasing the frequency of such heat waves.

Noticeable symptoms: The two serious conditions caused by exposure to heat differ in their symptoms as well as cause.

- *Heat exhaustion:* Sweat begins to pour from the skin, accompanied by weakness, dizziness, and perhaps fainting or vomiting. The skin is pale, cold, and clammy. Body temperature is normal or lower since the primary problem is insufficient electrolytes.
- *Heat stroke:* The victim feels very feverish but stops sweating; the temperature soars (often over 104°F), pulses pound. The person is confused or becomes unconscious. The skin is first flushed, then ashen or purple.

Treatment options: Each of the heat-related illnesses requires a different treatment.

- *Heat exhaustion:* Have the person lie down in a cool place with the feet elevated. Loosen clothing and sponge the face with cold water or, after a warning, spray the person lightly with cool water from a hose. Have the person drink a cool liquid, such as a "sports drink" or water containing a small amount of salt—do not have the victim chew or swallow salt tablets. The person may feel better quickly, but should take it easy. If the person is elderly or cannot keep the liquid down, he or she should be taken to a hospital.

Call ambulance

- *Heat stroke:* People with heat stroke usually need to be hospitalized. ***Call 911 or an ambulance immediately.*** While waiting for help, bring the victim's body temperature down as quickly as possible. If possible, wrap the victim in a wet sheet and use a fan to increase the rate of evaporation and cooling. Alternatively, put the person in a tub of cold water or sponge or spray the body with cold water.

Prevention: Young children and the elderly should take special precautions to avoid prolonged exposure to heat or direct sun on warm days, but everyone should be careful. Wear loose-fitting clothing and a hat, preferably one with a wide brim. Avoid strenuous outdoor activity during the middle of a hot day.

Heat stroke is an emergency that requires medical assistance as soon as possible. While waiting for an emergency vehicle, take steps to lower body temperature, such as placing a damp cloth on the forehead and wiping exposed parts of the body with a cooling liquid—alcohol, if available, cools faster than water.

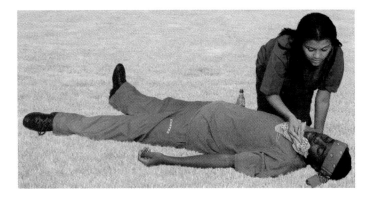

When exercising, rest in the shade for five to ten minutes every half hour, and drink lots of water even if not thirsty. Do not drink large amounts of alcohol in hot weather.

Hemophilias

(HEE-muh-FIHL-ee-uhs)

DISEASE

TYPE: GENETIC

See also
Blood
Genetic diseases
Von Willebrand's disease

On the Internet
MEDLINE PLUS
www.nlm.nih.gov/medlineplus/
hemophilia.html

Hemophilia is the name given to a group of several closely related hereditary diseases of the blood. The most common and best known are hemophilia A and hemophilia B. Hemophilia A occurs more often than hemophilia B and tends to have more serious effects.

All hemophilias have the same basic symptom, although there is great variation in severity: Blood does not clot properly. Minor wounds or surgery—even dental work—may cause excessive bleeding. Internal bleeding is even more dangerous, particularly if it occurs in the brain.

Those who are severely affected are at high risk for developing chronic arthritis. Spontaneous bleeding into the joints of the arms and legs inflames them, making them swollen and sore. Repeated attacks damage both bone and connective tissue and may eventually result in permanent crippling. Other potential complications include anemia from repeated blood loss, impaired vision from bleeding into the eye, and brain damage or even death from bleeding into the brain.

Cause: Blood clotting is brought about by two main agents: small, very flat bodies called platelets and a protein in blood plasma called fibrinogen (fiy-BRIHN-uh-juhn). When a wound occurs, platelets collect in the area of damage. Contact with air or with the edges of an internal break causes platelets to release chemicals that interact with fibrinogen. Fibrinogen then changes into an insoluble protein called fibrin (FIY-brihn). Fibrin forms a net of long fibers that traps blood cells, resulting in a clot.

Each step in this process uses chemical reactions involving specific proteins called factors. Different factors are labeled with Roman numerals, such as VIII (8) or IX (9). Hemophilias result when one or more clotting factors are absent, deficient, or defective, so that the sequence is disrupted. Hemophilia A is caused by an abnormally low level of factor VIII in the blood; hemophilia B from a low level of factor IX.

Hemophilias A and B are both X-linked diseases; that is, the genes that cause them are located on the X chromosome and they usually affect boys only (see Genetic diseases).

Incidence: Hemophilia A occurs in about one in ten thousand boy babies, and is seven times as common as hemophilia B.

Noticeable symptoms: Excessive bleeding, even from small cuts, and unusual susceptibility to bruising are likely to become apparent during infancy or early childhood. Internal bleeding from bruises may make a limb swell up and become painful for days at a time. Movements may become stiff as a result of bleeding and the formation of scar tissue in joints.

Treatment options: Severe hemophilias are treated by replacing deficient clotting factors. Concentrated factors are periodically injected: factor VIII for hemophilia A, factor IX for hemophilia B.

Mild cases of hemophilia A may not require clotting factor replacement. It is often possible to treat them with a synthetic pituitary hormone called desmopression, which improves platelet activity.

People with hemophilia should avoid certain drugs that aggravate bleeding. These include blood thinners such as heparin and warfarin (Coumadin) and NSAID painkillers such as aspirin and ibuprofen. Those affected should also *wear a medic-alert bracelet identifying the disease for prompt and appropriate treatment in case of an accident.*

Avoid aspirin

Medic alert

Hemophilus influenzae type B

(hee-MOF-ih-luhs ɪʜɴ-floo-EHN-zee)

Phone doctor

Hemophilus influenzae type B, or Hib, is a bacterium that can cause upper respiratory infection and lead to serious complications, such as meningitis, in unvaccinated babies and young children.

Cause: *Hemophilus influenzae* type B was so named because the bacterium was thought to cause influenza in humans when it was first identified in 1892. It does not. But Hib bacteria can cause meningitis, pneumonia, and bone, ear, and joint infections. Hib is usually spread by contact with a healthy person who is a carrier. It goes into the body through the mouth or nose, then enters the blood. Outbreaks can occur in crowded places such as day-care centers.

Incidence: Hib has been among the world's leading causes of illness in children and a frequent cause of death. Despite the existence of an effective vaccine since the late 1980s, the disease still causes 3 million serious illnesses annually, leading to nearly 400,000 deaths per year, nearly all among children under five. Children who survive are frequently left with permanent disabilities, such as deafness or lowered intelligence. But in the 90 or so nations that have introduced the vaccine, illness has fallen to low levels, and deaths have nearly disappeared.

Noticeable symptoms: The symptoms of Hib meningitis, the most serious complication of Hib infection, are fever, headache, sensitivity to bright light, stiff neck, vomiting, and convulsions.

Other Hib infections cannot easily be recognized at first. A sore throat or an earache that does not go away may be Hib. *All illnesses that continue for more than a week or ten days may be caused by bacteria or parasites and require treatment.* Unlike a common cold, mild influenza, or other mild viral diseases, untreated bacterial diseases, such as Hib infection, can persist or become much worse as they progress.

Diagnosis: If meningitis is suspected, a physician will do a spinal tap to get fluid that surrounds the brain and spinal cord. If the fluid is cloudy with pus in it, the cause is probably meningitis.

Treatment options: A child with Hib meningitis requires hospitalization and about 10 to 14 days of antibiotic therapy. In the case of other Hib-related complications, most of which are not life-threatening, the physician will prescribe an antibiotic that can be taken at home. It is important to take the full amount of the medicine to ensure that the bacterium is completely destroyed.

Stages and progress: Hib infection usually begins as an upper respiratory infection. Bacteria enter the bloodstream from the respiratory system and travel the blood to other parts of the body, including the coverings of the brain, or meninges. Meningitis is inflammation of the meninges. The onset of Hib meningitis is slow in some cases, rapid in others. If meningitis develops, the child is contagious and requires isolation. If meningitis is diagnosed and treated quickly, the child should recover in a few weeks. If there is a delay in diagnosis and treatment, complications may result, including deafness, blindness, and developmental disability (mental retardation).

Prevention and risk factors: The best prevention is immunization. All infants should begin Hib vaccination when they are two months old. Children 15 months to 5 years who have not been vaccinated should be evaluated on a case-by-case basis to determine if they should be vaccinated. Older children and adults are unlikely to become ill from Hib and so do not need to be vaccinated. Individuals who have not been vaccinated and who come into close personal contact with diseased persons may take antibiotics to prevent infection.

Get vaccinated

Hemorrhagic fevers

(HEHM-uh-RAAJ-ihk)

DISEASE

TYPE: INFECTIOUS (VIRAL)

On the Internet
MEDLINE PLUS
www.nlm.nih.gov/medlineplus/
hemorrhagicfevers.html

Certain viruses attack the circulatory system, causing internal bleeding (hemorrhaging), leaking of the capillaries, coma, and shock, all accompanied by fever; hence the general name for these diseases: hemorrhagic fevers.

Cause: Hemorrhagic fevers are caused by certain viruses. Among the most notorious fevers are Ebola, Lassa, Rift Valley, yellow, and dengue. American hantavirus disease and the African-based Marburg disease are also in this class. There is a high death rate from these diseases, which kill by causing uncontrollable bleeding throughout the body.

Various modes of transmission exist. Ebola is spread through contaminated blood and other body fluids, and by eating the meat of infected animals. Marburg is also spread through infect-

Emergency Room

ed meat. Yellow, Rift Valley, and dengue fevers are spread by mosquitoes. Lassa fever is carried by rodents, and hantavirus is in rodent droppings or saliva. In addition, Marburg disease and Lassa fever (as well as Ebola) can be spread person to person.

Incidence: Hemorrhagic fevers occur mainly in tropical and subtropical regions. Since the early 1990s there has been a resurgence of dengue fever and yellow fever, particularly in places with overcrowded living conditions, poor sanitation, and widespread poverty. Dengue fever has shown a tendency to expand its range, probably because of global warming. Lassa fever (1950s), Marburg (1967), Ebola (1976), and American hantavirus (1993) are recently detected emerging diseases.

Noticeable symptoms: Hemorrhagic fevers produce flulike symptoms, including fever, headache, fatigue, abdominal pain, nausea, vomiting, and cough. Within days of the onset of these symptoms the afflicted person may collapse and go into shock. *Immediate medical attention is essential if a hemorrhagic fever is suspected.*

Diagnosis: The doctor will review relevant medical history, such as recent travel to an area where a hemorrhagic fever is common. A blood sample will be examined for evidence of infection.

Treatment options: There are no known cures for these diseases. Treatment consists of relieving the symptoms. Such relief can often enable the body's own immune defenses to shake off the fever. In many cases people gradually recover, particularly if they were strong and in good health prior to infection.

Hemorrhoids

(HEHM-uh-ROIDZ)

DISEASE

TYPE: MECHANICAL

Hemorrhoids (*piles*) are a common form of varicose veins. Localized swellings of the veins appear either outside the anus (external hemorrhoids) or inside (internal hemorrhoids).

Cause: The most frequent cause of hemorrhoids is mechanical irritation, often from the pressure of hard stools passing through the anus. Hard stools are usually caused by constipation.

Hemorrhoids are especially prevalent during pregnancy, when blood vessels naturally expand and constipation is common.

They also can be a consequence of obesity, a sedentary lifestyle, including jobs that require constant sitting, or cirrhosis of the liver.

See also
Constipation
Rectum
Varicose veins

Phone doctor

On the Internet
NATIONAL DIGESTIVE DISEASES
INFORMATION CLEARINGHOUSE
digestive.niddk.nih.gov/ddiseases/
pubs/hemorrhoids/

Noticeable symptoms: Mild hemorrhoids may be unnoticeable. Those that are inflamed or contain blood clots may bleed or cause itching or pain. If the veins break, there will be bright red blood in the stool. *Notify your doctor if you observe blood coloring the water in your toilet bowel.*

Diagnosis: External hemorrhoids are usually visible, but internal ones may be observed only by stretching the opening of the anus with the fingers, observing the lower part of the colon with a tool called an anuscope or proctoscope, or examining the colon with a sigmoidoscope or colonoscope.

Treatment options: Hemorrhoid pain can sometimes be soothed simply with heat (warm baths or compresses) or cold (ice packs). Inflammation is often treated with rectal sprays, ointments, or suppositories containing a topical anesthetic and an anti-inflammatory drug. Hemorrhoids, especially mild ones, tend to shrink and heal by themselves. Only those that are severely inflamed or that contain blood clots require removal by a doctor.

Severe hemorrhoids can be cured by injecting a chemical that causes them to shrink, by *ligation* (binding them at the base until they wither away), freezing them with liquid nitrogen, or surgically removing them.

Prevention: Avoid constipation by eating foods that contain plenty of fiber, such as whole grains, fruits, and vegetables; drink plenty of fluids; and lose excess weight. Regular exercise is helpful. It is also wise to avoid straining when trying to move the bowels.

Hepatitis A and E

DISEASE

TYPE: INFECTIOUS (VIRAL)

Like other organs, the liver can become infected. The Latin for "inflammation of the liver" is *hepatitis*, hence the general name for such diseases. Infections specific to the liver tend to be viral, so most liver infections are properly termed "viral hepatitis." But chemicals such as carbon tetrachloride and alcohol can cause liver inflammation that is also "hepatitis." A few liver inflammations result from infections by a protozoan.

Several different viruses infect the liver. This entry concerns similar diseases caused by two viral agents that can spread through food or water, hepatitis A (sometimes known as HAV) and hepatitis E. Entries that follow cover other types of viral hepatitis.

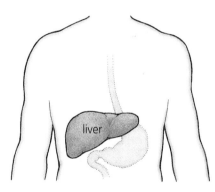

While most potentially infectious agents are killed by the strong acids of the stomach, some have found ways to survive a trip through the digestive system. The viruses that cause hepatitis A and E are able to move from the digestive system to the liver, where they take over cells and interfere with normal activities of the organ.

Phone doctor

Cause: Viruses that cause A or E hepatitis are transmitted in water or food. An infected person releases ("sheds") the virus in fecal matter, which can contaminate water supplies or food. Drinking contaminated water or eating the food exposes a person to the virus. Such fecal-oral transmission is known as *enteric* (ehn-TEHR-ihk), which means "intestinal."

In certain crowded conditions, especially with young children (as in a nursery school), hepatitis A can be transmitted directly from person to person, probably via unwashed hands after a bowel movement. Hepatitis A can also be transmitted directly from person to person by blood shared through contaminated needles, by deep kissing, or by anal sex.

Hepatitis E has the same general transmission modes and symptoms as hepatitis A, but a different virus causes the disease.

Incidence: Until recently hepatitis A cases in the United States may have been as high as 150,000 per year, although only about 25,000 of those were reported. With the introduction of an effective vaccine in 1995, the number of cases dropped dramatically. Today the number reported is about 7,500. Canada has lower totals, ranging between 500 and 1,000 per year. Worldwide, however, there may be as many as 2 million annual cases, taken together, of diagnosed hepatitis A or E. Hepatitis E occurs mostly in tropical regions.

Noticeable symptoms: The earliest symptom of hepatitis for many infected persons is jaundice, a yellowish cast to the skin or whites of the eyes caused by poor liver function. ***Anyone with noticeable jaundice should see a physician.*** Other symptoms include those similar to the "flu," such as nausea, loss of appetite, vomiting or diarrhea, and fatigue. Poor liver function can lead to clay-colored stools, dark urine, or pain in the region of the liver.

Diagnosis: Hepatitis A can be identified with a commercial blood test. Hepatitis E can be determined only with advanced blood tests not routinely available in the United States.

Treatment options: The main therapy for either hepatitis A or E is bed rest, although sometimes injections of gamma globulin (GLOB-yuh-lihn), a mixture of antibodies taken from donated blood, are used to mitigate symptoms and discourage

On the Internet
CENTERS FOR DISEASE CONTROL
AND PREVENTION (CDC)
www.cdc.gov/ncidod/diseases/
hepatitis

transmission. Alcohol puts an additional strain on the liver and should be avoided until symptoms subside.

Stages and progress: Hepatitis A is usually present for two to six weeks before any noticeable symptoms develop. As with most viral illnesses, after a time (often about six weeks for hepatitis) the immune system prevails, and all symptoms go away. Even then the virus remains for two or three weeks more. Transmission of the disease can occur any time when the virus is present, whether there are symptoms or not.

Prevention and risk factors: The main risk comes from eating unsanitary food or drinking contaminated water. If someone in the household is infected with hepatitis A or E virus, take precautions to avoid contaminated feces. Since 1995 a vaccine effective against hepatitis A has been available for use for children two and older. Anyone with hepatitis A or E should avoid contact with others to minimize the spread of the disease.

Hepatitis B

DISEASE

TYPE: INFECTIOUS (VIRAL)

On the Internet
CENTERS FOR DISEASE CONTROL
AND PREVENTION (CDC)
www.cdc.gov/ncidod/diseases/
hepatitis

The word *hepatitis* refers to any disease that causes inflammation of the liver. The most common cause of hepatitis is infection of the liver by a virus. Until the 1940s physicians thought that there was only one type of viral hepatitis. A second virus that produces hepatitis was discovered as a result of an accident. Although similar in symptoms to the previously known infection, the new form spread by a different route. Today the two types are called A and B.

Increasing ability to detect differences among viruses has led researchers to identify several different viral liver infections, all called *hepatitis*. Hepatitis C is very common and the subject of the next entry. Hepatitis D is not a disease-causing virus by itself but makes infections with B worse. For that reason some physicians prefer to call it "the delta factor" instead of D. Hepatitis E is more like A than it is like the others.

Cause: The virus that causes hepatitis B—also known as HBV—is transmitted primarily by infected blood or during unprotected sex, although mothers sometimes transmit it to children shortly after birth.

A person cannot contract hepatitis D without already having hepatitis B infection. Hepatitis D, or the delta factor, consists almost entirely of nucleic acid lacking the usual viral coat. The hepatitis D virus needs to use the outside coat from a hepatitis B virus to infect cells, so it is a cofactor of that disease.

Incidence: Hepatitis B in the United States has been on the decline, with only about 8,000 new cases reported annually. The principal reason for this decline has been an effort since 1999 to ensure that all Americans 18 and younger have been vaccinated against the disease. Despite the decline, over a million Americans have chronic hepatitis B infection and are carriers of the disease. Some 4,000 to 5,000 Americans die annually from the disease.

Worldwide, 350 million persons are thought to be chronically infected; 500,000 to 750,000 die from the disease annually.

Since hepatitis B is transmitted not only by blood products but also sexually, it can infect a population that is more geographically spread out than the small groups that often develop hepatitis A from a single source. Hepatitis B, for example, becomes rampant in the male homosexual community during periods in which there is a great deal of promiscuity.

Noticeable symptoms: For many, the earliest symptom of hepatitis is jaundice, a yellowish cast to the skin or whites of the eyes caused by poor liver function. Other symptoms include those similar to "flu," such as nausea, loss of appetite, vomiting or diarrhea, and fatigue. Poor liver function can lead to clay-colored stools, dark urine, or pain in the region of the liver.

Although half of all infections with hepatitis B cause no symptoms at all, infection can lead to serious complications later, even when not symptomatic at first.

Diagnosis: Hepatitis B and hepatitis D can each be identified by a commercial blood test.

Treatment options: For all forms of hepatitis bed rest is the main treatment. If dehydration becomes a problem, a patient may be put into the hospital for intravenous administration of liquids. If the liver is severely inflamed, steroids may be injected. The antiviral Iamivudine, often used for HIV infection, is also effective against hepatitis B. Alpha interferon is also helpful.

For any liver disease alcoholic beverages are harmful, espe-

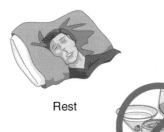

Rest

Avoid alcohol

cially if combined with the pain reliever acetaminophen (Tylenol is a common brand).

Stages and progress: Infection with hepatitis B can be mild and fairly short-lived in many cases, although an incubation period with no symptoms can be from one to six months. As with most viral illnesses, after a time the immune system prevails, and the infection ends. In 5 to 10% of all patients, however, disease symptoms go away, but the virus continues to infect liver cells, a condition called *chronic*. Chronic hepatitis can lead to the scarring of the liver called cirrhosis. Severe cirrhosis interferes with liver function and can lead to death. Hepatitis B is also thought to cause liver cancer in a fairly high percentage of cases.

In some cases hepatitis has no further effect on the human host, but the virus is able to spread to other humans. Perhaps as many as a million Americans are carriers of hepatitis B.

Sometimes liver function is badly compromised, and the disease takes a sharp turn for the worse. Acute hepatitis (from any cause, including chemical poisoning as well as any of the various viral infections) is known as *fulminant* (FUL-muh-nuhnt) *hepatitis*—fulminant means that it occurs suddenly and intensely; it may affect the brain, resulting in coma or even death. Hepatitis B can become fulminant or occur as an acute attack. For a person with both the B and D viruses the probability of fulmination or cirrhosis is enhanced over the chances for a person with B only.

Prevention and risk factors: Since 1991 the vaccine for hepatitis B has been recommended as part of the standard series of vaccinations for all newborn children. Adults who because of lifestyle or because they are traveling to a location where hepatitis B is common also can protect themselves with vaccination. Mothers who have hepatitis B nearly always transmit it to their children, but this risk can be reduced with vaccination of the baby at birth and treatment with immune B globulin.

The risk factors for hepatitis B are similar to those for AIDS, with sexual transmission, especially among homosexual men, common, as well as transmission in blood between drug users sharing needles. Hepatitis B reaches perhaps as many as 80% of the homosexual population.

Blood transfusions are no longer a risk for contracting hepatitis B because the blood supply is monitored for the virus.

Known exposure to hepatitis B virus may be treated with immune B globulin to prevent the disease, although treatment must be carefully monitored since the blood fraction can sometimes provoke severe allergic reactions.

History: In the first half of the twentieth century physicians recognized that hepatitis is spread by contaminated water in much the same way as cholera is. During World War II, however, a major outbreak of serious hepatitis led to the discovery of another mode for transmission of the disease. A vaccine intended to protect American troops against yellow fever had to be withdrawn quickly when the vaccine was found to be the cause of the hepatitis outbreak. The vaccine had been made from human blood products. Research into this kind of hepatitis after the war can be counted—along with deliberate exposure to radioactive substances, experimental nontreatment of syphilis, and administration of psychedelic drugs to unsuspecting personnel—as one of the serious abuses of research in the name of science. Children with Down syndrome and prisoners were deliberately injected with infected blood to determine the cause and progress of the newly discovered form of hepatitis.

As a result of these experiments, however, physicians recognized the two different viruses that infect the liver by different routes, hepatitis A spread primarily through contaminated water and food and hepatitis B spread through sex or blood. When tests revealed that there were many cases of hepatitis that were not caused by either A or B, other causes of the disease were recognized.

Hepatitis C

DISEASE

TYPE: MECHANICAL

In 1990 a test was developed for hepatitis C virus (HCV), a blood-borne virus that causes infection of the liver. In 1992 more than 300,000 letters were sent to people who had received blood transfusions and organ donations who might have been infected with HCV. Today HCV infection is one of the most common diseases transmitted by blood.

Cause: HCV is one of a family of viruses that can cause serious liver damage. In some cases HCV infection can be fatal. HCV

On the Internet
CENTERS FOR DISEASE CONTROL
AND PREVENTION (CDC)
www.cdc.gov/ncidod/diseases/
hepatitis

damages the liver, causing scarring (cirrhosis); in time HCV can lead to cancer. There is no vaccination to prevent this and no drug to cure it.

Incidence: An estimated 2.7 million persons in the United States and 300,000 Canadians are infected, and perhaps as many as 200 million worldwide. Most of these individuals developed the disease as a result of sharing needles for injected drugs.

Hepatitis C can be passed from an infected pregnant woman to her baby, but this happens in only 1 to 5% of cases. It is safe for an infected woman to nurse her newborn baby.

There are an estimated 8,000 to 10,000 deaths in the United States each year as a result of complications of hepatitis C.

Noticeable symptoms: Symptoms of HCV infection include loss of appetite, severe fatigue, fever, nausea, jaundice (a yellowing of the eyeballs and skin), and dark yellow urine. About 50 to 70% of those who test positive for the hepatitis C virus have no symptoms at all. Nearly everyone becomes chronically infected, however. In many cases symptoms are mild: fatigue, nausea, and weight loss. Others develop cirrhosis of the liver or liver failure.

Diagnosis: Hepatitis C infection is often identified through routine blood tests. These tests include some for the virus and some that tell how well the liver is working. If these preliminary liver tests are abnormal, further tests are done to find out if HCV is present. A test called a liver biopsy is also done to see if there is liver damage. In a biopsy a small piece of the liver is removed and examined microscopically.

Treatment: Vaccination for hepatitis A and hepatitis B, which could further damage the liver, is usually recommended as soon as HCV infection is diagnosed. Further treatment usually occurs only after the extent of liver damage is determined. Interferon alone or interferon in combination with another antiviral drug, such as ribavirin, is used for treatment. People with other serious illnesses, such as HIV/AIDS or kidney disease, are usually not given these medications. The treatment lasts six months to two years and has serious side effects, including flulike symptoms, depression, and rashes. Many people are unable to complete the treatment because of the side effects. Women cannot take HCV treatment during pregnancy.

Progress and stages: Some people with hepatitis C infection become ill very quickly. But in most infected people symptoms of infection take 15 to 30 years to develop. Many of these individuals will live a normal lifetime without severe complications. Some, however, will develop severe liver disease or liver cancer. It is thought that some people with HCV infection will never become ill.

Risk factors: A history of injection drug use, long-term kidney dialysis, and receipt of a blood transfusion, blood products, or an organ transplant before 1992 are the major risk factors for HCV infection. Although HCV infection can be deadly, it is not spread through everyday activities or through coughing, sneezing, hugging, food, water, or sharing of eating utensils.

Prevention: The nation's blood supply is carefully tested for hepatitis C, so transfusion-related HCV infection is now rare. The most important method of prevention is to avoid sharing needles to inject drugs. But the disease can be spread by sharing other drug paraphernalia, toothbrushes, and razors. Needles used for body piercing and tattooing might also transmit HCV, but there are no cases related to these practices in the United States. Sexual transmission is rare, but people who have many sex partners should use condoms to prevent the spread of HCV. People infected with hepatitis C who are in monogamous relationships with individuals who are not infected do not have to use condoms.

If there is any concern that a person is infected, he or she should be tested to avoid infecting others.

History: Scientists working with hepatitis B in the 1960s found many puzzling cases of liver disease that seemed to be different from hepatitis B; these are now assumed to be largely hepatitis C. The timing suggests that the disease came into being or became widespread in the 1950s, coinciding with a major wave of intravenous drug use in the United States. There is evidence that hepatitis C did not exist or was at least rare before this time. Stored blood samples from World War II fail to test positive for the disease.

In 1975 some patients who got blood transfusions developed a form of hepatitis that the tests for both hepatitis A and B failed to recognize, so this form came to be called nonA, nonB hepatitis at first. The virus for nonA, nonB hepatitis became known as hepatitis C after it was isolated in 1987 and its genome sequenced in 1990.

Don't share needles

Hernias

DISEASE

TYPE: PHYSICAL DISORDER

See also
Diaphragm
Heartburn
Testes

On the Internet
KIDS HEALTH
kidshealth.org/teen/
sexual_health/guys/hernias.html

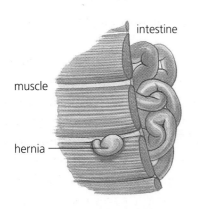

The most common forms of hernia occur when part of an intestine pokes through the wall of muscles that surrounds the abdomen (belly).

A hernia is any condition in which part of an internal organ protrudes through an abnormal opening. Although heavy lifting is popularly thought of as the cause of hernias, many hernias have other origins. Some people are born with openings in the abdominal muscles, for example, so that nothing more than a cough can produce a hernia at the weak spot. Babies may be born with hernias.

Cause: Thin sheets of muscle hold most internal organs in place. Part of an organ pushing through a weak spot or a rip in surrounding muscle is a hernia. For example, the stomach bulging up through a weak spot in the diaphragm is called a *hiatal hernia,* a common condition among people over 60.

The most familiar hernias occur in the groin area, where the abdominal wall meets the thighs. These *inguinal hernias* occur when part of the intestine pushes through the muscle wall. In men there are small openings in that wall that permit passage of a cord that tethers the testes to their blood supply. If these openings are too large, the condition is often described as a *congenital weakness* in the muscle wall. Even with larger-than-normal openings a man may reach adulthood before a hernia appears. What finally causes the intestine to push through is not always apparent. Sometimes men tear abdominal muscles through lifting too much weight or lifting improperly.

Though women sometimes get inguinal hernias, they are much more likely to suffer *femoral hernias.* Here part of the intestine pushes down the canal carrying the femoral artery into the thigh.

Infants sometimes have *umbilical hernias.* Part of the intestine bulges through the abdominal wall at the point where the umbilical cord attaches. This condition usually corrects itself as the baby grows.

Incidence: Hiatal hernia is very common in older people, with incidence increasing from about 10% for those under 40 to about 70% for those over 70. Men are most likely to get other forms of hernia, and inguinal hernias account for about three-quarters of all instances. Overweight and pregnant women are more likely than other women to suffer femoral hernias. Of all hernia types, the femoral is most likely to produce dangerous complications.

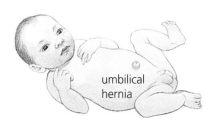

Hernias are named by the place through which they poke. A baby's umbilical hernia is truly at the belly button, but an umbilical hernia in an adult is in the weak region around the belly button.

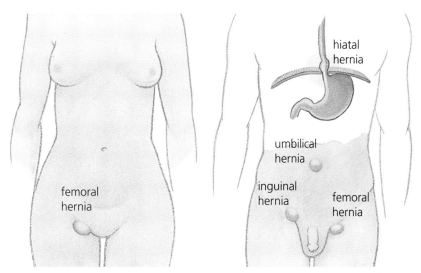

A femoral hernia in men or women, but more commonly in women, is where the femur joins the pelvis, that is, at the top of the thigh. Men have inguinal hernias where the tube that carries semen passes through the abdominal wall.

Phone doctor

Emergency Room

Noticeable symptoms: Sudden discomfort when lifting heavy objects or bending over can signal a hernia. A telltale sign is a small, soft lump under the skin in the groin area. *Get medical attention as soon as possible after you notice a lump in the groin area.* Sometimes there is little pain in this early stage. The hernia will often be *reducible,* meaning the intestine can be gently pushed back in place by a physician, making the lump disappear.

Sometimes abdominal hernias push through at a point where they protrude into the scrotum. Called an *indirect inguinal hernia,* this type can be very painful and may make the scrotum swell.

Inguinal and femoral hernias left untreated can be extremely dangerous. Normally, when the intestine pushes through the abdominal wall, the opening tends to get narrower behind it. If the opening gets small enough to cut off the blood flow to the intestinal bulge, the hernia is said to be *strangulated.* Blood flow must be restored quickly to prevent gangrene from developing.

If you have a hernia that abruptly grows larger and will not go back into place, it probably has become strangulated. Usually, there is sharp pain and nausea with a strangulated hernia, but for the elderly especially there may be no pain. *Get immediate medical help when a hernia becomes strangulated.* An untreated strangulated hernia may result in death.

Hiatal hernias may be the cause of symptoms of heartburn and chest pain, although in many cases they produce no symptoms at all.

Diagnosis: Physicians' training often enables them to find small hernias during physical exams, even before their patients have noticed them. Most men are familiar with the part of a physical exam in which the physician lays a finger on a particular spot in the groin and asks the patient to cough. The spot is where there is a tether between the testicle and the body, a tether that passes through the abdominal wall. That opening is the site of the inguinal hernia, if it exists. Coughing increases pressure on the lower abdomen and pushes the intestine into the abdominal wall, where it will poke through if the opening for the tether is too large.

Treatment options: Doctors may recommend wearing trusses and corsets to keep a hernia from getting larger. But abdominal (inguinal) hernias generally do not heal by themselves. Surgery is the preferred treatment.

Hiatal hernias that produce no symptoms do not need treatment. About one case in twenty, where the hernia is especially large, requires surgery.

Prevention: The best ways of avoiding an abdominal hernia

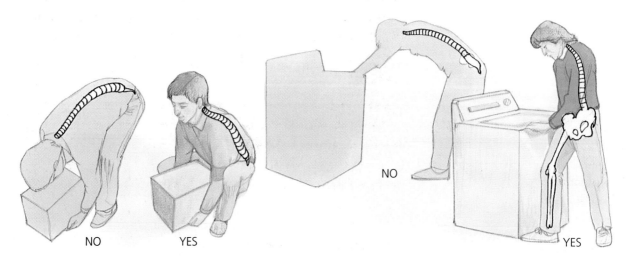

NO   YES   NO   YES

Although we associate heavy lifting with back pain, it also can provoke a hernia. The main precautions, however, protect the back and also help prevent hernia. Don't lift too much at one time, and put the strain on leg muscles when you can.

are to keep in good physical shape and to take sensible precautions when lifting heavy objects. Do some stretching exercises first to loosen up the abdominal muscles. Do not bend over and lift with your back. Instead, squat down and, keeping your back straight, lift with your legs. If you have not been lifting heavy objects for a long time, get someone to help. If you have a congenital weakness of the abdominal wall, precautions like these may help delay or even prevent the getting of a hernia.

Herpes	*See* **Cold sore; Genital herpes**
Herpes zoster	*See* **Chicken pox; Shingles**
Hiatus hernia	*See* **Heartburn; Hernia**
Hiccups	*See* **Diaphragm**
High blood pressure	*See* **Hypertension**
Histoplasmosis	*See* **Fungus diseases**

HIV and AIDS

DISEASE

TYPE: INFECTIOUS (VIRAL)

See also
Anemias
Cancers
Cryptosporidiosis
Dementia
Epidemics
Lymphocytes
Opportunistic diseases
Pneumocystis carinii **pneumonia**
STD (sexually transmitted diseases)
Tuberculosis

The human immunodeficiency virus (HIV) may live in a person for years without causing disease. If undiagnosed and untreated, it eventually begins to destroy the person's immune system, causing the disease called acquired immunodeficiency syndrome (AIDS). HIV/AIDS is among the world's most serious medical problems, now resulting in millions of deaths annually.

Cause: HIV is a retrovirus, a type of virus that contains an enzyme called reverse transcriptase, which enables the virus to replicate in a host cell. There are two main strains of HIV: HIV-1 and HIV-2. They are much alike, with similar modes of transmission and similar associated infections. However, in people with HIV-2, immunodeficiency develops more slowly and is milder than in people with HIV-1. HIV-2 is found primarily in Africa while HIV-1 can be found around the world.

HIV is spread through contact with infected body fluids such as semen and blood. Almost all infections result from one or both of two behaviors: when two people have sex without

Did You Know?

It is a myth that only homosexuals have to worry about HIV and AIDS. Heterosexual intercourse is the main mode of HIV transmission worldwide.

using a condom, or when they share needles to inject drugs, steroids, or other substances.

HIV infects, reproduces in, and eventually destroys white blood cells called T-4 lymphocytes, whose function is to help other lymphocytes produce antibodies to fight disease. The destruction of the T-4 lymphocytes leaves the body vulnerable to infection by other disease-causing organisms.

Incidence: AIDS was discovered in 1981. It spread rapidly around the world, resulting in an epidemic that has had a profound impact on families, communities, and nations.

Worldwide, an estimated 40.3 million people are infected with HIV. The epidemic continues to grow, with almost 5 million people infected in 2005. Sub-Saharan Africa is hardest hit; two-thirds of those infected—some 25.8 million—live in this area.

In 2005 more than 3 million people died of HIV-related illnesses, including 2.4 million in sub-Saharan Africa. Of the total, more than 500,000 were children.

More than 900,000 cases of AIDS have been reported in the United States since 1981. Currently, more than 1 million Americans are believed to be living with HIV/AIDS, with about 25% undiagnosed and unaware of their infection. Over 530,000 Americans have died from AIDS since the epidemic began.

Education and prevention efforts have helped reduce HIV infection rates in certain groups, such as young people in Uganda, injecting drug users in Spain, and men who have sex with men in Western nations.

Noticeable symptoms: A person with HIV may remain without symptoms for a dozen years or more after infection. Although seemingly healthy and able to lead a normal life, it is important to note that during this time the person is infectious—that is, he or she can spread HIV to other people.

Early AIDS symptoms are easily mistaken for those of other viral infections. They may include fever, night sweats, unexplained weight loss, headache, fatigue, enlarged lymph nodes (glands of the immune system), and persistent or frequent oral or genital yeast infections.

Diagnosis: In addition to persons who have suspicious symptoms, those who are sexually active or who inject drugs should be tested regularly for HIV/AIDS. An HIV antibody test is performed to determine if the immune system is making antibodies to fight HIV. If HIV antibodies are present, the person is HIV-infected (HIV positive). A physician then takes blood to learn the person's T-4 lymphocyte count. Because the number of T-4 cells declines as HIV infection progresses, the count gives the physician an indication of the patient's status. The physician also tests blood to determine viral load, that is, the amount of virus in the blood. This information helps the physician determine how fast the infection is progressing.

Treatment: Treatment depends on the stage of the disease and on how fast the infection is progressing. Medications introduced in the mid-1990s greatly improved the outlook and way of life for HIV-positive people who have had access to these drugs.

Two types of medications, called antiretrovirals (AAN-tiy-REHT-roh-VIH-ruhlz) and protease (PROH-tee-ays) inhibitors, are used to slow the progression of HIV in the body. Typically, these medications are used in combinations, often called an AIDS cocktail or HAART (highly active antiretroviral therapy). Despite their effectiveness, the medications have serious side effects in some people, including anemia, pancreatitis, and disturbances of fat metabolism. In addition, drug-resistant strains of HIV have evolved.

Stages and progress: HIV gradually weakens the immune system—a process that can be slowed for decades with early, sustained treatment. With sufficient destruction of the immune system, however, the body becomes unable to fight off infections that a healthy immune system can control. The person, who now has AIDS, becomes prey to opportunistic infections—disorders that have the opportunity to thrive when the immune system is depressed. It is these secondary diseases that eventually cause death in HIV-infected people.

One opportunistic infection common among AIDS patients is Kaposi's sarcoma, a rare form of cancer previously seen only in elderly men. Another is *Pneumocystis carinii* pneumonia, a rare parasitic disease of the lungs. Additional secondary diseases include cytomegalovirus retinitis (SIY-tuh-MEHG-uh-loh-VIY-ruhs REHT-uhn-IY-tihs), which often destroys vision; cryptosporidiosis, an intestinal infection that reduces the ability to

Because HIV is transmitted only by bodily fluids, and then only when the virus enters the bloodstream, you cannot contract AIDS from touching an infected person. Hugging and touching bare skin are both perfectly safe, but unprotected sexual activity or contact with blood is extremely risky.

absorb nutrients; and tuberculosis of the lungs, bones, or other body organs.

One condition—AIDS dementia—is caused by the HIV infection itself. If not checked by medication, HIV may infect the brain and destroy brain cells. People with AIDS dementia lose some motor control and may have a shuffling gait. They may also become easily confused and experience feelings of paranoia.

Prevention: The best prevention is to not use drugs and to abstain from sexual intercourse, or to have sex only when certain that one's partner is not infected with HIV. The next best prevention is to use a condom correctly with every partner, every time, for vaginal, oral, and anal sex. For people who use needle drugs, the best prevention is to not share needles, syringes, or other drug paraphernalia.

In a small percentage of cases, people have received infected blood during a transfusion. Today in North America and other developed places, all blood and blood products are tested to prevent transmission in this way. Another route of transmission occurs when a baby is born to an HIV-positive woman. Treatment with antiretroviral drugs during pregnancy and delivery, however, greatly reduces transmission to newborns.

Health officials at all levels of government—from individual communities to those working with the World Health Organization—point out that many people are dying unnecessarily as a result of ignorance, misinformation, and insufficient prevention, testing, treatment, and care programs. Education about HIV and AIDS and access to basic prevention services are considered critical to limiting further transmission of the virus.

Hives

SYMPTOM

Hives—also known as *wheals* or as *urticaria* (UR-tih-KAIR-ee-uh) —refers to a serious rash, one that is red or pink, raised or bumpy, and itchy. The well-defined pink welt is called a hive or a wheal. The bumps are raised because *histamine,* usually produced in reaction to an allergen, expands tiny blood vessels just under the skin and releases lymphatic fluid, which collects under the skin. The color is produced by the expanded blood vessels.

There are two basic types of hives: *acute,* which usually last for a few hours and go away in less than a day; and *chronic,* which last for weeks or, in severe cases, occur periodically for

Phone doctor

years. Each individual welt lasts less than one day, but in chronic cases new hives appear daily. At some point in their lives some 15 to 20% of people develop hives, usually of the acute type.

Parts affected: Any part of the skin may be affected by hives. ***If face, eye, or throat begins to swell, see your physician promptly.*** A slight swelling that reduces breathing after exposure to an allergen may cut off breathing altogether on the next exposure.

Associations: Allergies such as hay fever, eczema, and *dust-mite allergy* are the most likely causes of hives. Hives are sometimes triggered by an allergic reaction to a drug, such as penicillin or even aspirin. Bee or wasp stings frequently cause hives. Stress can cause hives in certain people; for example, a student facing a particularly tough exam may break out in hives.

The cause of chronic hives is often difficult to establish. In rare cases hives are a symptom of a more serious disease, such as "lupus" (systemic lupus erythematosus), hepatitis, or cancer.

Prevention and possible actions: Avoid the specific foods that cause you problems. To identify the problem-causing foods, remove suspects from the diet, and reintroduce them one by one.

Relief of symptoms: Over-the-counter antihistamines may relieve symptoms completely for a time but may induce sleepiness. Modern nonsedating prescription antihistamines can be taken daily, preventing hives in people who are subject to frequent attacks. Even a cool shower can reduce itching.

Hodgkin's disease

DISEASE

TYPE: CANCER

Hodgkin's disease is a form of cancer characterized by painless swelling of lymph tissue. It is a special type of lymphoma. Other lymphomas are generally called *non-Hodgkin's lymphomas*.

Cause: The root cause of Hodgkin's disease is unknown, but many investigators suspect an infectious agent such as a virus. Some people appear to have a genetic susceptibility to the disease.

Incidence: About 7,400 Americans are diagnosed annually with Hodgkin's lymphoma. Adults account for 85 to 90% of cases, children 10 to 15%. Although it can develop at any time, it is most likely to strike two age groups: age 15 to 40 and after age 55. The disease is slightly more common in males than females.

On the Internet
LYMPHOMA INFORMATION
NETWORK
www.lymphomainfo.net/
hodgkins

Did You Know?
Hodgkin's disease was first described by Thomas Hodgkin in 1832, but not named after him until 1865 when the disease was rediscovered.

Noticeable symptoms: Enlargement of lymph nodes, particularly in the neck or armpits, is an early sign of Hodgkin's disease. Other common symptoms include fatigue, night sweats, weight loss, severe itching, and fever that comes and goes over a period of several days or weeks.

Diagnosis: A doctor will conduct a thorough physical examination, take blood samples, and, if Hodgkin's is suspected, perform a lymph-node biopsy. The lymph tissue will be viewed under a microscope; the presence of large, multinucleated cells, called Reed-Sternberg cells, indicates Hodgkin's disease. The greater the number of these cells in lymph tissue, the more aggressive the disease. Once the diagnosis is confirmed, additional tests, such as a bone marrow biopsy or body scan, may be performed to learn how to best treat the disease.

Treatment options: If the disease is limited to lymph nodes in one region, radiation therapy is typical. Chemotherapy is administered if the disease has spread through the body. The chemicals attack cancer cells vigorously but are less toxic to other cells.

If untreated, Hodgkin's disease is fatal. With early treatment most people are cured completely. Even in advanced cases, the five-year survival rate is about 60%. For people under age 20 with Hodgkin's lymphoma, the five-year survival rate is 93%.

Hookworm

DISEASE

TYPE: PARASITIC

People who walk barefoot in moist tropical and subtropical areas, particularly where sanitation is poor, can be infected with hookworms. Although medicine is available to rid the body of the infestation, most victims are unable to afford treatment.

Cause: Hookworm disease is caused by either of two separate species of hookworm. Each of these small roundworms has a similar complex life cycle. Adult worms live attached to the walls of a person's small intestine, where they feed on blood. After mating, the female worms produce thousands of eggs. These pass out of the body with the feces. The eggs hatch into larvas, which can penetrate human skin. The larvas travel via blood and lymph to the lungs, crawl up the trachea, and are swallowed. Once in the intestines, they mature, and the cycle begins again.

Sometimes larvas enter the body through the mouth. This is

most likely to occur with young children who play in the dirt, then put unwashed fingers on their mouth or food.

Incidence: Hookworm infection is most common in the tropics and subtropics, especially in poor rural areas. There currently are an estimated 740 million cases, with the highest prevalence in sub-Saharan Africa and eastern Asia. In the United States hookworms are found in the Southeastern region.

Noticeable symptoms: A rash called "ground itch" may develop on the skin at the spot where the larva penetrated. Many people do not exhibit any signs of infection. Others experience abdominal pain and diarrhea. Fatigue, weakness, and pale skin color may indicate that the worms have caused anemia. Untreated hookworm in children can retard physical or mental growth. Symptoms are more severe if there has been infection by multiple worms. For babies it is sometimes fatal.

Diagnosis: If a doctor suspects hookworms, a stool sample will be examined under a microscope for eggs, and a blood test will be done for anemia.

Treatment options: An antiworm medication will be prescribed. Iron supplements may be given if anemia is present.

Prevention: Hookworms can be avoided by wearing shoes in infected areas. Wash hands and clean under fingernails after playing or working with soil; better yet, wear sturdy gloves when working with soil.

Hormonal system

BODY SYSTEM

Hormones are chemicals made in the body that travel through the blood to regulate body functions or achieve specific tasks. Many have familiar names, such as insulin, estrogen, testosterone, or growth hormone, while others are less well known to the general public, such as cholecystokinin (CCK).

Glands: Many hormones are produced by organs called *glands*. Some hormones are produced by organs that have other purposes as well and are not considered glands. For example, the stomach, the heart, and the small intestine all produce important hormones.

For the most part glands come in two varieties—those that release their hormones into the blood and those that release their secretions through tubes called *ducts*. Glands that release hormones into the bloodstream form the endocrine system, while those that have ducts to release fluids are called exocrine glands. Secretions of exocrine glands are not considered hormones. Some glands, such as the pancreas, have both endocrine and exocrine functions. The exocrine glands are all part of the digestive system.

Increasingly, hormones are available either as products of genetic engineering (human insulin and human growth hormone, for example) or as synthetics (the notorious steroids used for body building are synthetic testosterone and close relatives). Such manufactured hormones offer both the promise of relief from hormone-deficiency diseases and the possibility of hormone abuse.

Main human hormones

Hormone	Associated gland(s)	Function
Adrenalin (epinephrine)	Adrenal medulla	Increases blood sugar, pulse, and blood pressure
Adrenocorticotropic hormone (ACTH)	Anterior pituitary	Stimulates adrenal cortex
Aldosterone	Adrenal cortex	Controls reabsorption of sodium and potassium by the kidneys
Calcitonin (thyrocalcitonin)	Thyroid	Lowers level of calcium in blood by inhibiting calcium release from bones
Cholecystokinin (CCK)	Glands in small intestine	Stimulates pancreatic secretions, contraction of gallbladder, and intestinal movements
Chorionic gonadotropin	Placenta	Stimulates ovaries to continue producing estrogens and progesterone during early stages of pregnancy; is detected in a pregnancy test
Corticotropin-releasing factor (CRF)	Hypothalamus	Causes adrenals to produce hormones
Cortisol and related hormones	Adrenal cortex	Affects metabolism of proteins, carbohydrates, and lipids
Estrogens	Ovaries and placenta	Stimulate development of secondary sexual characteristics in females; help regulate ovaries and uterus during menstrual cycle and pregnancy
Follicle-stimulating hormone (FSH)	Anterior pituitary	Stimulates follicle development in females and sperm production in males
Gastrin	Glands in stomach	Stimulates secretion of gastric juice
Glucagon	Pancreas (islet cells)	Increases blood sugar level by stimulating breakdown of glycogen
Growth hormone (somatotropin or somatotrophic hormone; STP)	Anterior pituitary	Stimulates bone and muscle growth

(continued)

Hormone	Associated gland(s)	Function
Insulin	Pancreas (islet cells)	Lowers blood sugar level and increases storage of glycogen
Luteinizing hormone (LH)	Anterior pituitary	Stimulates ovulation and formation of corpus luteum in females and testosterone production in males
Nerve growth factor (NGF, or p75)	Brain	Necessary for growth of brain cells
Norepinephrine	Adrenal medulla	Increases metabolic rate and constricts blood vessels
Oxytocin	Produced in hypothalamus, stored in posterior pituitary	Causes sex to be pleasurable; stimulates uterine contractions during childbirth and milk release; promotes bonding with children in females of some mammal species and may help regulate social interactions in human females
Parathormone (parathyroid hormone or PTH)	Parathyroid	Increases level of calcium in blood by increasing calcium release from bones; decreases blood phosphate
Progesterone	Ovaries and placenta	Helps regulate uterus during menstrual cycle and pregnancy
Prolactin (lactogenic hormone or LTH)	Anterior pituitary	Stimulates milk production (lactation)
Secretin	Glands in small intestine	Stimulates secretion of pancreatic digestive juices
Testosterone (androgens)	Testes	Stimulates development of male sex organs and secondary sexual characteristics; supports sperm production
Thyroid-stimulating hormone (TSH)	Anterior pituitary	Stimulates thyroid gland to produce and secrete thyroxin
Thyroxin (thyroxine)	Thyroid	Controls rate of metabolism and growth
Vasopressin	Produced in hypothalamus, stored in posterior pituitary	Controls reabsorption of water by kidneys (antidiuretic); increases blood pressure; causes parental or sexual bonding in males of some mammals; may affect social interaction in human males

Hormone disorders

Hormones are chemical messengers produced mainly by small organs scattered throughout the head, neck, and trunk that together form the endocrine system. The organs, called endocrine glands, are not physically connected to each other, but interact as a system by releasing hormones into the blood. The bloodstream carries hormones to every cell in the body. The endocrine system combines with the nervous system to regulate the main functions of the body—reproduction, growth, and production of energy.

Too much or too little: Some hormones are necessary for life. The rest are necessary in proper amounts for good health. Any condition that results in too much or too little of a given hormone interferes with growth or metabolism.

Physicians use the prefixes *hyper-* and *hypo-* to describe the level of a hormone. A mnemonic, or way to remember the meaning, of the prefix is to associate the "oh" sound in *hypo-* with the "oh" sound in *low*. If you are told that your condition is *hypothyroidism*, you have low thyroid function, or not enough thyroid hormones. But *hyperthyroidism* is high, or too much, thyroid hormone.

Many of the combinations of symptoms that result from incorrect amounts of hormones have specific names and are described in the table below. The most common disorders—the three forms of diabetes—are covered in separate entries in addition to the brief descriptions here.

Reproduction and hormones: The word *hormones* in a non-medical context usually refers to sexual desire. This association is not far off the mark. Low testosterone, a hormone associated with males but also found in females, leads to a lowered interest in sex.

Other reproductive hormones control the sequence of events that allows a woman to conceive a child. These hormones—three released by the pituitary as well as hormones from the ovaries—direct reproduction. Incorrect amounts of the hormones generally lead to infertility. Adjusting the amount of female reproductive hormones is the main action of birth control pills, used to produce temporary infertility.

Common hormone disorders

Medical name	Hormone problem	Symptoms
Achondroplasia	Too little growth hormone produced by pituitary	Short stature, relieved by genetically engineered growth hormone
Acromegaly	Too much growth hormone produced by pituitary; often the result of a tumor, which can usually be removed or reduced with radiation	In middle age, hands and feet keep growing; eventually, bones and skin thicken and diseases develop, including hypertension and possibly diabetes mellitus
Addison's disease	Too little of hormones produced by outer part of adrenals (adrenal cortex), especially aldosterone and cortisol; one possible cause is too little ACTH being produced by pituitary	Weakness, fatigue, brown spots on skin, weight loss, low blood pressure, and gastrointestinal problems

(continued)

Medical name	Hormone problem	Symptoms
Cretinism	Too little thyroid hormone in early infancy; often prevented by regular use of iodized salt	Short stature, developmental disability, large tongue, navel hernia, and poor muscle coordination
Cushing's syndrome	Too much of hormones produced by outer part of adrenals (adrenal cortex), especially aldosterone and cortisol, because of too much pituitary activity	High blood sugar levels and "moon face" combined with fat pads and overweight; lowered sex hormone levels, muscle wasting, water buildup, and sometimes emotional changes; skin may thin and minor infections may become severe and long-lasting; children may stop growing
Diabetes insipidus	Too little antidiruretic hormone (ADH) produced by pituitary	Urine passes in large amounts, relieved by synthetic ADH
Diabetes mellitus, types 1 and 2	Too little insulin produced by pancreas or inability of cells to use insulin	Sweet urine in large amounts and high glucose levels in blood; various complications are common
Graves' disease	Too much of hormones produced by thyroid, often because thyroid is enlarged	Nervousness and hyperactivity, sweating, hand tremor, fatigue, breathlessness, palpitations, heat intolerance, stomach and intestinal spasms, weight loss, and blurred or double vision; not all symptoms necessarily occur
Hashimoto's thyroiditis	Too little hormone produced by thyroid because it is under attack by immune system	Visible swelling of thyroid gland (goiter)
Hypoglycemia	Too much insulin (perhaps as result of tumor or overadministration in diabetes) or too little cortisol is produced by adrenals	Sweating, racing pulse, tremors, headache, anxiety, confused thinking, fainting
Hypopituitarism	Too little of six hormones normally produced by front lobe of pituitary; one result is too little thyroid, adrenal, and gonad hormone production	Goiter, fatigue, infertility, amenorrhea in women; short stature if condition starts in childhood
Hypothyroidism	Damage to thyroid gland; often an autoimmune problem; results in too little thyroid hormone	Cretinism in infants; in adults, fatigue, easily corrected with thyroid-stimulating medicines; severe cases are myxedema (see below)
Myxedema	Too little production by thyroid	Swelling caused by too much fluid; hoarse speech, yellowish skin, and personality changes
Parathyroidism	Parathyroids produce too much hormone, often as result of benign tumor	Excess calcium circulates in blood, where it can cause kidney stones; bones weaken because calcium is taken from them
Pheochromocytoma	Too much epinephrine and norepinephrine produced by adrenals, probably as result of benign tumor	Panic attacks with little or no known cause

Huntington's disease

DISEASE

TYPE: GENETIC

On the Internet
NATIONAL INSTITUTE
OF NEUROLOGICAL DISORDERS
AND STROKE
www.ninds.nih.gov/disorders/
huntington/huntington.htm

Did You Know?
Woody Guthrie, author of the song "This Land Is Your Land, This Land Is My Land," died from Huntington's disease—a disease first described in 1872 by George Huntington, a 22-year-old American physician.

Huntington's disease is a hereditary disorder that primarily affects the brain and nervous system. Nerve cells, or neurons, in certain areas of the brain gradually deteriorate, so that the brain no longer operates normally. Two functions are particularly affected: the control of voluntary movement, or motor control, and the mental faculties of perception, memory, and thought.

Huntington's disease cannot be cured or stopped. Its course is prolonged, with symptoms gradually worsening, often over a period of 10 to 30 years. The first signs of the disease usually do not appear until the age of 35 to 45. At that age many affected individuals have already had children, and may have passed on to them the abnormal gene that causes the disease.

Cause: Huntington's disease is caused by a single abnormal gene on chromosome four. It is a *dominant gene* (see Genetic diseases). Any person who has the gene will inevitably have the disease. And any child of that person has a one-in-two chance of inheriting the gene and the disease.

The normal gene *huntingtin* in chromosome four contains the short, three-element sequence denoted CAG in its DNA, which codes for the protein huntingtin. The sequence CAG calls for a specific amino acid within the protein. Sometimes a mutation occurs that causes CAG to be repeated more than once. If the number of repeats is less than 28, there is no adverse affect. If the number is between 29 and 34, the individual inheriting the gene will not have the disease, but there is a substantial risk that the number of repeats will be even larger in the offspring of that person. If the number is between 34 and 39, the individual runs a slight risk of having the disease and, again, a substantial risk of an even larger number in his or her offspring. If the number of repeats is 40 or more, the individual inheriting the gene will certainly have defective huntingtin protein, which produces the disease.

This pattern of increasing numbers of repeated DNA sequences from one generation to the next, eventually resulting in an abnormality, occurs in some other genetic disorders as well. The most notable is fragile-X disease.

Huntingtin apparently interacts with other gene products in forming certain body tissues but does not remain distinguishable by itself. The effects of the abnormal form of it are mysterious; no one knows why these are concentrated in certain areas of the brain—particularly the basal ganglia that control movement and the cerebral cortex, which controls the mental processes of cognition. It is known, however, that the higher the number of repeated CAG sequences in the mutated gene, the earlier Huntington's disease will appear and the faster it will progress. Those with very high numbers of repeats are more likely to suffer juvenile Huntington's disease, which becomes apparent before age 20 and usually results in death within 10 years.

Incidence: Huntington's disease is uncommon. It occurs somewhere between 1 in 10,000 to 25,000 births. But it tends to be concentrated within certain populations and families.

Noticeable symptoms: The first "sign" of the disease is family history. Like all disorders caused by dominant genes, Huntington's disease is inherited in a direct line from parent to child. Ordinarily, one cannot have the disease unless a parent had the repeated CAG sequences and a grandparent had them, and so forth.

The first symptoms of the disease usually do not appear until mid-adulthood. By that time the affected person may already have had children without being aware of possessing the abnormal gene. Furthermore, the first symptoms are likely to be subtle and easily overlooked—slight clumsiness of movement, say, or mild absentmindedness, or increased moodiness. The characteristic breakdown of motor control and loss of mental capacity may take months or years to become unmistakable.

Sometimes these symptoms are erroneously thought to result from alcoholism, especially if the person developing Huntington's disease is also a heavy drinker. People with Huntington's run a risk of being arrested for "drunkenness" when observed staggering, slurring words, and behaving oddly.

Abnormal motor control may first appear as stiffness, clumsiness, or unsteadiness, particularly in walking. But then most affected persons become subject to a wide variety of involuntary movements: jerks, twitches, and a distinctive writhing or flailing of the arms and legs. From this repetitive writhing and flailing the disorder gets its traditional name—*Huntington's chorea* (kaw-REE-uh), from an old Greek word meaning "dance."

Control of the mouth and tongue muscles is also damaged.

Speech becomes slurred and unintelligible. Eventually sufferers cannot walk, talk, stand, or manage simple manual tasks.

Mental signs begin with irritability, forgetfulness, or depression. Like the physical symptoms, these moods and lapses get progressively worse. In the final stages affected persons are likely to become disoriented and demented.

Diagnosis: The repetitions in the gene make the disease relatively easy to identify through DNA analysis. Thus it can be diagnosed genetically long before any symptoms appear. The abnormal gene can be found in the cells of all affected individuals, even those of unborn fetuses. Furthermore, calculating the number of CAG repeats makes it possible to predict how early the disease will make its appearance and how fast it is likely to progress.

Treatment options: There is no specific treatment for Huntington's disease, but a variety of medications and techniques are used to alleviate its symptoms and preserve normal function for as long as possible. Antipsychotic drugs, for example, may help control involuntary movements, and antidepressants and other mood-changing drugs may be used to relieve the mental and emotional impact of the disease. Regular exercise can help those affected feel better physically and mentally, and good nutrition can help make up for the enormous expenditure of energy caused by involuntary movements.

Hydrocephalus
(HIY-droh-SEHF-uh-luhs)

DISORDER

TYPE: GENETIC;
      DEVELOPMENTAL;
      INFECTIOUS

Hydrocephalus is a disorder known familiarly as *water on the brain*. The "water" is cerebrospinal (SEHR-uh-broh-SPIY-nuhl) fluid, which is constantly produced in hollow chambers called *ventricles* deep within the brain. Normally, the fluid circulates around the brain and spinal cord and is eventually reabsorbed into the blood. If the fluid gets blocked or is not properly reabsorbed, it builds up in the ventricles, making them swell. The pressure is transmitted through the brain to the skull, causing the head to enlarge.

The chief danger of hydrocephalus is brain damage, which results in death or neurological problems such as developmental disability (mental retardation), epilepsy, or cerebral palsy. If the condition is diagnosed and treated early enough, such complications can often be avoided.

Emergency Room

normal position
of bones of skull

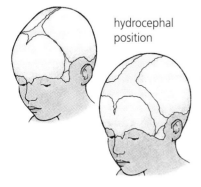

hydrocephal
position

At birth the bones that form the skull are not completely connected, but they usually grow together as a person ages. If there is hydrocephalus, however, the pressure inside the skull increases the separation and the skull becomes larger than normal.

Cause: Hydrocephalus may be congenital (developed before birth) or acquired. Congenital hydrocephalus may be inherited in genes from parents or be a result of chromosomal abnormalities. It is associated with developmental disorders such as neural tube defects. It may also be caused by an infection, such as rubella, toxoplasmosis, or syphilis, transmitted from the mother to the fetus before birth. In addition, it may result from bleeding into the ventricles at or near the time of birth.

Acquired hydrocephalus can occur at any age. It can be caused by infections such as bacterial meningitis, by brain tumors or cysts, or by brain injuries, especially those that produce bleeding (hemorrhaging) within the skull.

Incidence: Congenital, or infantile, hydrocephalus affects about 1 in every 1,000 births. The incidence of acquired hydrocephalus in not known.

Noticeable symptoms: The most obvious sign of hydrocephalus in infants is enlargement of the head, which may be apparent at birth or develop later. This results from a baby's skull not having completely fused into a single bone so that internal pressure pushes the parts outward. In adults symptoms can include vomiting, headaches, unusual irritability or lethargy, and downward deviation of the eyes ("sunset eyes"). ***These symptoms require immediate medical attention.***

If the head enlargement occurs before birth, it may be visible by ultrasound. The diameter of the head is routinely measured in all examinations from birth onward to check for enlargement. Internal examination of the brain using a CT or MRI scan can reveal enlarged ventricles.

Treatment options: The standard treatment is a surgically inserted *shunt*, a slender plastic tube that drains the excessive fluid from the ventricles. One end is inserted into a ventricle through a small hole in the skull; the rest is implanted under the skin, extending into the body—most often opening into the cavity of the abdomen. A valve in the tube ensures that fluid flows in the proper direction. The shunt remains in place indefinitely. As the child grows it must be periodically lengthened, repaired, and replaced.

Prevention: For adults and older children, wearing protective headgear in sports is especially important.

Hypertension

Did You Know?

Although in ordinary English the word *essential* means "necessary," essential hypertension is high blood pressure whose cause is unknown. It is the most common type of high blood pressure.

As blood flows through the arteries, it presses against the arterial walls. When this force, or pressure, is consistently stronger than normal, you have *high blood pressure,* or hypertension.

Cause: Blood pressure rises and falls with every beat of the heart. It is usually measured by two numbers, such as 120/80, read as 120 over 80. Maximum pressure is exerted when the heart contracts and pumps blood into the arteries. This is the systolic (sih-STOL-ihk) pressure, the higher of the two numbers. Blood pressure lowers to its minimum when the heart rests between contractions. This is the diastolic (DIY-uh-STOL-ihk) pressure, the lower number. Normal blood pressure is a reading below 120/80 when the person is at rest. Pre-hypertension exists if systolic blood pressure is consistently between 120 and 139 or diastolic blood pressure is between 80 and 89. A higher reading of either number indicates hypertension.

Blood pressure depends on several factors. These are the volume of blood that has to be pushed through the blood vessels, the flexibility of artery walls, and the ease with which blood can pass through the arteries. These determine how hard and fast the heart must pump. Blood pressure is also influenced by hormones and the nervous system.

These factors are affected by what a person is doing and feeling. It is normal for blood pressure to vary throughout the day. It increases when a person is physically active, worried, excited, or frightened. It decreases when that person is calm, at rest, or asleep. With hypertension, however, blood pressure is consistently elevated regardless of activities or emotions.

Physicians are unable to determine an underlying cause for most cases of high blood pressure. In 10% of the cases a specific disease or condition is responsible. Kidney disease, hormone disorders, pregnancy, and certain medications such as birth control pills or cortisone constitute some of the causes.

Incidence: More than 50 million Americans have hypertension. It is a major risk factor for cardiovascular disease, stroke, and kidney failure. In the United States it is associated with some 500,000 strokes and 1.2 million heart attacks annually. However, almost 50% of people with hypertension are either unaware of their disease or are aware but not being treated for it.

Children and young adults may have hypertension but prevalence increases sharply with age. Approximately three out of five men over 75 and three out of four women over 75 have the disease. African Americans are twice as likely to develop hypertension as Caucasians. Death from hypertension also is much more prevalent among African Americans.

Noticeable symptoms: Hypertension may not produce any symptoms. Untreated hypertension, however, speeds up hardening of the arteries. Advanced hypertension usually causes damage to the heart, kidneys, or eyes and can produce a stroke. These may be the first signs of hypertension.

Phone doctor

An occasional measurement showing elevated blood pressure does not necessarily imply hypertension. Physical activity, nervousness, smoking, or drinking coffee or cola just before blood pressure measurement is taken often produce elevated readings. Many people also exhibit "white-coat hypertension" in the doctor's office. ***When pressure is consistently above 120/80, a person should discuss the problem with a physician.***

Diagnosis: The physician will measure blood pressure using a sphygmomanometer (SFIHG-moh-muh-NOM-ih-tuhr) and a stethoscope. A rubberized cuff is wrapped around the upper arm. Air is pumped into the cuff so that it tightens around the arm and stops the flow of blood. The physician places the stethoscope on the lower arm inside the elbow and listens for sounds in the artery as air is let out of the cuff. A tapping sound is heard as blood flows back into the artery. The systolic pressure is then read from a mercury gauge, a round dial, or a digital display. More air is released, and when the tapping sound disappears, the diastolic pressure is read. If blood pressure readings are high, the physician will use other tests and procedures to determine whether the heart, kidneys, or other organs show any damage.

Avoid salt

Exercise

Don't smoke

Treatment options: Many physicians use a "stepped-care" approach in treating hypertension. In the first step the patient is instructed to adopt various lifestyle changes. These may include losing weight, reducing salt intake, exercising regularly, limiting alcohol, and ceasing to smoke. If hypertension is mild or moderate, these measures may be sufficient to lower pressure and keep it controlled.

If this does not work, drug therapy will be required. Different drugs eliminate excess salt or fluid (diuretics), slow down the heart (beta blockers), or relax heart and artery muscle tissue by preventing the production of body chemicals that constrict or squeeze blood vessels. These include ACE (angiotensin-converting enzyme) inhibitors and calcium channel blockers. Many newer drugs need to be taken only once each day and have few or no side effects in most people (older drugs frequently caused impotence, diarrhea, or dizziness). If the first drug your physician prescribes does not work, a different dosage or a different drug will be tried, or perhaps two or three drugs in combination.

With the appropriate medication for hypertension, blood pressure usually returns to normal and stays that way. Most people who take medication to control hypertension must continue to do so for the rest of their lives. ***Do not stop taking the medication unless a physician tells you to.*** Blood pressure may rise to a dangerous level if medications are discontinued abruptly or other complications may arise.

A physician will also treat any underlying cause of hypertension that can be found. However, in most cases the cause of hypertension is not known. Physicians call high blood pressure with no known cause *essential hypertension*—but hypertension may be a symptom of a kidney or heart disorder. If that is the case, there is no need for continuing medication when the condition that caused hypertension has been corrected.

Stages and progress: Hypertension is often called a silent killer because it produces no symptoms until it is already well advanced. Untreated hypertension is the leading cause of stroke and a major factor in heart failure, kidney failure, and heart attack. Keeping blood pressure at a normal level lowers the chance of developing one of these serious, often fatal conditions.

Prevention: It is good practice for adults to have a blood pressure check at least once a year. A person cannot change family medical history or age but can control most of the other risk factors for hypertension: tobacco and alcohol use, obesity, high levels of salt or fat in the diet, lack of exercise, and stress. Where stress cannot be avoided, relaxation techniques such as meditation and regular mild exercise minimize its effects.

See **Goiter**

Hypertrophic cardiomyopathy

(HIY-puhr-TROH-fihk KAHR-dee-oh-miy-OP-uh-thee)

DISEASE

TYPE: GENETIC

See also
Arrhythmias
Cardiac muscle
Circulatory system
Congenital heart defects
Genetic diseases
Heart

Hypertrophic cardiomyopathy, or HCM, is a disease of the heart muscle. The muscle fiber of the left ventricle becomes abnormally thickened, or *hypertrophied*. Blood flow through it may be impaired, and attacks of arrhythmia (irregular heartbeat) may occur, especially during or after exertion. HCM is notorious for causing the sudden and unexpected deaths of young athletes.

Incidence: HCM is relatively uncommon and varies widely in its severity, so its incidence is hard to measure. One estimate is as high as 1 in 500; another, as low as 1 in 10,000.

Cause: HCM is strongly familial; that is, it is concentrated in certain families, although there is no evident pattern of genetic inheritance. Even though the disease is considered to be inherited, its effects usually do not show up until the growth spurt of adolescence.

Noticeable symptoms: Many who have HCM are aware of no symptoms at all. Observable symptoms can be caused by hypoxia, a lack of sufficient oxygen in the blood, shortness of breath, weakness or fatigue, dizziness or fainting, and chest pain (angina). People sometimes experience palpitations—an unusual awareness of one's own heartbeat. Sudden death is a relatively rare but devastating consequence.

Diagnosis: HCM may be suggested by a heart murmur audible through a stethoscope or by an abnormal electrocardiogram. But the surest way to diagnose it is with a form of ultrasound called an echocardiogram.

Treatment options: Many people are only mildly affected and need no treatment at all. The most common form of treatment is with medications, such as beta blockers or calcium channel blockers, that make the heart work less hard, and antiarrhythmic drugs that help prevent irregular heartbeat. Some benefit from the insertion of a pacemaker to improve the efficiency of the heart. Those who are seriously affected may need surgery to improve blood flow through the heart. Those believed to be at high risk for life-threatening arrhythmia may have an automatic defibrillator implanted in their bodies. This device administers an electric shock to the heart in the event of an attack. In very rare instances a heart transplant may be advisable.

Those affected run a higher than normal risk of endocarditis, an infection of the heart lining, and should take preventive antibiotics before undergoing surgery or dental treatment.

Hypertrophy
(hiy-PUHR-truh-fee)

SYMPTOM

Hypertrophy is an abnormal increase in the *size* of any part of the body due to an increase in the size of the cells making up that part. Similar to but distinct from it is *hyperplasia* (HIY-puhr-PLAY-zhuh), which is an enlargement of a bodily part due to an increase in the *number* of normal cells making it up.

Hyperplasia occurs in a developmental defect of the adrenal glands, but for the most part the body responds to a felt need for additional tissue by hypertrophy.

Hypertrophy usually occurs in response to need. If some part of the body begins to fail, healthy tissue will grow in response and take up some of the work done by the failing part. Thus hypertrophy can be a healthy response. Hypertrophy produces muscle enlargement from exercise and growth of the uterus during pregnancy. And when one kidney has had to be removed by surgery, the other kidney enlarges.

Parts affected and symptoms: In other cases the underlying problem that caused hypertrophy represents a serious disorder. In hypertrophic cardiomyopathy, enlargement of a portion of the heart muscle, for example, the affected heart may not pump blood efficiently, causing difficulty in breathing or palpitations. This condition can be fatal. The prostate in men is frequently subject to hypertrophy; this can interfere with urination. The cause for this enlargement of the prostate, often confusingly called hyperplasia, is unknown.

One type of *arthritis* (osteoarthritis) of the joints involves a common form of hypertrophy. By the age of 40 almost all persons appear to evidence some arthritic deterioration in the joints bearing the bulk of their bodily weight. By age 70 virtually everyone is believed to have at least intermittent symptoms of arthritic pain and stiffness in at least some joints. Men on the average seem to develop such symptoms at earlier ages than women. Both cartilage and bone in the joints give rise to arthritic symptoms. And all tissues in and adjoining arthritic joints enlarge through hypertrophy.

A number of very rare diseases also exhibit hypertrophy. For example, *Dejerine-Sottas disease* appears in childhood, causing parts of the nervous system to grow larger. It is at first marked by increasing weakness and loss of sensation in the legs. *Virginal hypertrophy* refers to sudden overdevelopment of breasts in girls at puberty.

Relief of symptoms: Obesity, often caused by a combination of hypertrophy and hyperplasia of fat cells, is a serious health risk. While lifestyle changes can eliminate most obesity, other instances of destructive hypertrophy may require surgery. For example, virginal hypertrophy may require breast reduction, arthritic joints may need to be replaced with artificial ones, and an enlarged prostate may need to be surgically reduced to facilitate urination. Hypertrophic cardiomyopathy that does not respond to medication can also be treated surgically.

Hypoglycemia
(HIY-poh-gliy-SEE-mee-uh)

DISEASE

TYPE: CHEMICAL

Under normal conditions the nervous and endocrine systems work together to maintain a fairly steady level of sugar in the blood. But in hypoglycemia blood sugar drops abnormally low.

Cause: In hypoglycemia either not enough blood sugar is being produced, or too much sugar is being removed from the blood. Liver disease, stomach surgery, and certain medications can

On the Internet

NATIONAL DIABETES INFORMATION CLEARINGHOUSE diabetes.niddk.nih.gov/dm/ pubs/hypoglycemia

Eat sweets

prevent sufficient production of blood sugar. Sometimes the condition occurs as a complication during pregnancy. A bout of heavy drinking of alcohol can produce hypoglycemia, especially if nothing is eaten at the same time.

Malfunctions of endocrine glands can also cause hypoglycemia. For example, a tumor on the pancreas may cause overproduction of insulin, leading to excessive removal of sugar from the blood. People who take insulin to control diabetes mellitus—a disorder marked by too much blood sugar—are susceptible to hypoglycemia. If they take too large a dose of insulin or do not take it at the proper time, too much sugar may be removed from the blood.

Some people experience a temporary lowering of their blood sugar level several hours after eating a meal high in carbohydrates. This condition can often be corrected by lowering the sugar content of meals, since high sugar content in the blood triggers the glucose control mechanism, lowering it far too much in persons with this form of temporary hypoglycemia.

Noticeable symptoms: Early symptoms include faintness, sweating, weakness, nervousness, and rapid heartbeat. If the blood sugar level remains abnormally low for a prolonged period, the nervous system becomes impaired. Mental confusion, headaches, and hallucinations may ensue. Without treatment the situation may lead to convulsions and, in extreme cases, coma.

Diagnosis: A doctor will take blood samples and test blood sugar levels to confirm a diagnosis of hypoglycemia. The next step will be to determine the underlying cause.

Treatment options: An episode of hypoglycemia can be quickly dealt with by eating sugar; this is why people with diabetes mellitus should always have juice, sugar lumps, or candy at hand.

Hypotension

SYMPTOM

As blood flows through the arteries, it presses against the arterial walls. If this pressure is significantly lower than normal, the condition is called hypotension or low blood pressure. It is the

On the Internet
MEDLINE PLUS
www.nlm.nih.gov/medlineplus/
ency/article/003083.htm

Did You Know?
Two numbers usually measure blood pressure: maximum pressure and minimum pressure (when the heart rests between contractions). For most people the normal blood pressure range is between 90/60 and 120/80.

Phone doctor

Call ambulance

opposite of hypertension or high blood pressure. As a result of hypotension, too little blood flows to the brain, heart, and other vital organs.

Cause: The most common type is orthostatic hypotension, which can occur when a person suddenly changes body position, when standing up after lying in bed or after sitting in a chair. Orthostatic hypotension may also be a symptom of a central nervous system problem, irregular heartbeat, or dehydration—for example, it can occur during physical activity if a person is not taking in enough water and salt to replace that lost through perspiration.

Alcohol and various medications—including diuretics, heart medicines, and those used to treat high blood pressure—can cause hypotension. So can medical problems such as heart failure, heart attack, advanced diabetes, a severe allergic response, shock, and Addison's disease (in which the adrenal glands produce insufficient amounts of hormones that regulate blood pressure).

Symptoms: Dizziness or lightheadedness is the most obvious symptom of sudden orthostatic hypotension. Symptoms of low blood pressure that develops over time may also include unsteadiness, weakness, fatigue, fainting, and blurred vision. *When these symptoms persist, consult a physician.*

A sudden drop in blood pressure, as from substantial loss of blood, is called shock. Other symptoms of serious, immediate concern may include chest pain, shortness of breath, irregular heartbeat, headache, or severe upper back pain. *If a person is unconscious or exhibiting symptoms of a heart attack or another imminently fatal disease, an ambulance should be called at the very first symptoms.*

Treatment: Treatment depends on the cause of the low blood pressure and its seriousness. Hospitalization may be necessary, particularly in emergencies. If medications are determined to be the cause, their dosages may be altered. Internal bleeding, as from an ulcer, will be repaired. If the cause cannot be identified, a medication that raises blood pressure may be prescribed.

Hypothermia

(HIY-puh-THUR-mee-uh)

DISEASE

TYPE: MECHANICAL

See also
Alcoholism
Dementia
Diabetes mellitus, type 1
Diabetes mellitus, type 2
Fever
Heart failure

On the Internet
MAYO CLINIC
www.mayoclinic.com/health/
hypothermia/DS00333

Call ambulance

Body temperature usually remains at a healthy norm between 96°F and 100°F. But prolonged exposure to cold can cause body temperature to fall dramatically, with potentially fatal results.

Cause: Hypothermia develops when the body's control mechanisms are unable to maintain a steady body temperature. This can occur when a person is exposed to cold for several hours or to a cool, wet environment.

Incidence: The elderly are at particular risk of hypothermia. As a person ages, the internal mechanism that detects changes in body temperature becomes less sensitive. Also, older bodies are less able to maintain an even temperature even during warm weather.

For different reasons the very young may also experience hypothermia—small bodies cannot retain heat as well.

Heart disease, malnutrition, alcohol abuse, and *diabetes* can increase the risk of hypothermia. Various medications, including sedatives and tranquilizers, also increase the risk.

Noticeable symptoms: Signs of hypothermia include low body temperature, shivering, pale skin, drowsiness, lethargy, slowed breathing, loss of coordination, and mental confusion. The onset of symptoms usually occurs gradually, and the patient may be unaware of the loss of mental and physical ability. ***If you suspect that someone has hypothermia, seek immediate medical help. Hypothermia is a life-threatening condition if not promptly treated.***

Treatment options: First aid includes moving the person into a warm room, removing wet clothing, and covering him or her with a warm blanket. Do not expose the victim to high heat, however. If the person is conscious, warm nonalcoholic drinks without caffeine should be provided. If no pulse can be detected, or the person has stopped breathing, resuscitation must be initiated.

In the hospital the person may be placed in a warm bath. Various body processes, including heartbeat, are monitored. In extreme cases dialysis with warm salt solutions (removing the blood from the body and warming it) may be needed.

Prevention: It is advisable to visit older people regularly during cold weather to ensure that they eat well, have sufficient warm clothing and blankets, and keep their homes well heated.

INDEX

The first digit in **boldface** is the volume number; page numbers follow the colon.
Page numbers in **boldface** indicate entries.

Our thanks to the following organizations and persons who
made the photographs used in this set possible:

Christ Episcopal Church Youth Program (Mary Millan)
Maryknoll Lay Missioners (Jean Walsh)
Mount Vernon Teen Task Force (Chris Webb)
Putnam Family Support and Advocacy, Inc. (Pam Forde)

Photography assistant: Tania Gandy-Collins

MODELS
Roland Benson, Diana Brenner, Sally Bunch, Deirdre Burke,
Kevin Chapin, Michael Clarke, Michelle Collins, Bryan Duggan,
Germaine Elvy, Eugene Ehrlich, Caitlin Faughnan, Irmgard
Kallenbach, Max Lipson, Lydia McCarthy, Amanda Moradel,
Joshua Moradel, Veronica Moradel, Kate Peckham, Sara
Pettinger, Micaela Rich, Mario Salinas, Heather Scogna,
Halima Simmons, Wendy Sinclair, Barbara Totten, T.J.
Trancynger, Rolando Walker, Jean Walsh, Hannah Walsh-
Regotti, Maria Walsh-Regotti, Deborah Whelan, Gregory
Whelan, Francis Wick, Elaine Young, Leanne Young